The Sultan of Spring

THE SULTAN OF SPRING

BOB SAILE

*A Hunter's Odyssey Through
the World of the Wild Turkey*

Illustrated by Eldridge Hardie

THE LYONS PRESS

Printed in the United States of America

10 9 8 7 6 5 4 3 2 1

Design by Joel Friedlander Publishing Services, San Rafael, CA

Illustrations by Eldridge Hardie

Library of Congress Cataloging-in-Publication Data

Saile, Bob.
    The sultan of spring: a hunter's odyssey through the world of the wild turkey / by Bob Saile.
        p.   cm.
    ISBN 1-55821-625-1
    1. Turkey hunting—Anecdotes. I. Title.
SK325.T8S35   1998
799.2'4645'0977—dc21   97-26411
                                                      CIP

Portions of this book appeared in different form in *Field & Stream* magazine under the titles "The Name of the Gobbler Game," "High Noon Gobblers," and "Bird of Purgatory."

DEDICATION

To Carol, loyal, long-tolerant, and loving spouse, who doesn't hunt but understands why others do—and who prepares an elegant turkey dinner.

Contents

ACKNOWLEDGMENTS

Thanks go to Doug Harbour and his father, the late Colonel Dave Harbour, for introducing me to the world of the wild turkey; to Carroll Lange and Bill Hlavachick of the Kansas Department of Wildlife and Parks for their help with research on the restoration of wild turkey populations in Kansas; to Mary Kennamer of the National Wild Turkey Federation for statistical information and other assistance; to Slater Saile and Kerwin Lumpkins for their help in printing out the manuscript; and to all the turkey hunters who have shared time, hunting spots, and expertise with me in the spring turkey woods. And finally, obviously, to the bird itself.

INTRODUCTION

HUNTING IS A BLOOD SPORT, much more so than fishing, or at least the way in which fishing has evolved in the last half of the twentieth century. Though some of us who call ourselves hunters may want to eschew it or sugarcoat it, it is still a blood sport. And that basic fact is at the bottom of the chasm that separates the hunter from the nonhunter, or from the antihunter.

Those who do not hunt and consider it barbaric differ in many ways from those of us who do hunt, but chief among the differences is that the antihunter does not consider himself to be a part of nature. He rejects the reality that modern man is still part and parcel of the predatory chain and was, at one time, as wild and free as the animals he now hunts for sport. The true hunter seeks to return with his modern implements to that long-ago time, however briefly, and the culmination of that revisitation is achieved in the death of an animal or bird taken under challenging, fair-chase conditions. Or as close to fair as we can make them with our rules and regulations while not eliminating the possibility of a kill. The antihunter views nature from the outside, without touching it, as if peering through the glass of a museum display. The hunter seeks to get inside the glass and to become part of the display.

The hunter aspires to connect with and possess his quarry, and in most, if not all, forms of hunting that is ultimately achieved with a well-earned, well-deserved kill. I believe that what sets turkey hunting apart from some other forms of hunting is that the possession can occur with or without a kill, not because we "release" the quarry as in, say, catch-and-release trout fishing, but because for the time that we engage the bird on the ground with our calls and our strategy, he is ours whether he escapes or not, whether we succeed in killing him or not. In fishing, the linkage to the wild side of existence is in the strike and the feel of life at the end of the rod and line; the linkage in turkey hunting is achieved through the sight and sound of the biggest, strongest, and most elusive feathered creature in the woods. The wonder of it is that we are able, albeit with the assistance of the tools of hunting-related technology, to choreograph the connection.

There may be turkey hunters who are satisfied just to call in a gobbler and then let it walk or run away. With no apologies or guilt, I wish to make clear that such an approach is not my frame of reference, or the frame of reference of most of us who have joined the steadily growing ranks of those who hunt the wild turkey. Rather, I speak of the magic moments when we have established, in effect, a dialogue, a liaison, with the bird, and in so doing have created a communion, the outcome of which is uncertain. What happens after that is gravy. If the bird escapes us, our disappointment is tempered and, ultimately, erased by our affection, awe, and respect.

When the hunter succeeds and the bird has been killed cleanly and swiftly, a momentary regret enters the mind—a regret that the life is gone from this beautiful, wild creature. There is always, always, respect. Without it we are killers, not hunters. But there is no remorse in the heart of the true hunter if the kill has been accomplished within honest, ethical, and demanding limits. There should be exhilaration, not guilt. That is a paradox that those who do not choose to hunt, and who consider hunting barbaric, can never comprehend. As author Tom Kelly wrote in his classic little book, *Tenth Legion,* which has served for many of us as a kind of philosophical bible for the religion called turkey hunting: Hunters who no longer wish to kill need only stop hunting.

I would respect anyone who did that. Just as I respect anyone who never has hunted and thinks it is wrong. What I do not respect is the person who thinks it is wrong and insists that I think the same thing. There is a disturbing trend among some people in America these days not to be satisfied with their own beliefs unless that way of thinking can be forced on everybody else. This perversion of freedom of thought and speech sometimes masquerades under the guise of political correctness. Having the right to disagree is not enough for these folks: They arrogantly demand to mold the rest of us in their image.

The one thing I would never try to do in this or any other book or essay would be to force my views, of turkey hunting or anything else, on anybody. My mission here, if there is one that can be fairly construed as noble, is twofold. I would like to share with the hunter who is already engaged in this wonderful sport we call turkey hunting some of my joys, my triumphs, my failures, my observations, my insights (to whatever extent they are useful), my delights, and my adventures and misadventures in my own turkey hunting, as well as to share my acquaintance with some of the fascinating places and captivating personalities I have had the privilege to visit, meet, and know through turkey hunting. Most of all, I wish to entertain. To me, there is no such thing as a surfeit of literature on turkey hunting, and reading a good story on the subject is somewhat like enjoying the subtle, casual-contact preliminaries in a budding love affair: It ain't the real thing, the intimacies are yet to come, but it will do just fine until the real thing materializes. I firmly believe that imagination and anticipation are at least half the thrill.

And somehow something special, something crazy, something remarkable or funny or even spiritual, seems to happen with regularity in the world of turkey hunting, more so than in other areas of outdoor sport. Each encounter with the wild turkey adds to the growing body of the lore.

This book was also written for the hunter or would-be hunter who has managed, as I did for far too many years, to miss climbing aboard the turkey-hunting bandwagon. In this modest work of written words I want to steer the wagon straight up to his door and park it long enough for him to jump in and join the ride. There is plenty of room, and we will be off to a beckoning horizon of habitats where the wild turkey roams and where we can engage him on his own ground—mostly on his terms. And for a fleeting, heady, cosmic slice of eternity, make our connection with him.

We can possess him, for a brief time we can be a part of him, whether the gun is fired or not.

Let the wagon roll.

Bob Saile
Denver, Colorado

FOR LOVE OF THE GAME

I DIDN'T HAVE TO OWL-HOOT. Daylight was still only a silver-tinted promise back over my shoulder on the horizon, where rolling, brushy hills climbed away from the Beaver River, the source of the North Canadian. But even before I sat down, a gobbler roosted on the other side of the knoll in front of me, his aggressiveness triggered by the dirgelike calls of half a dozen real owls, sounded off with gusto.

Another gobbler joined in, and then another. These western Oklahoma toms were finally starting to talk, after two days of total silence. There had been much speculation back in camp about the why of this lockjaw. The prevailing theory was that this state wildlife area's prolific population of coyotes had taught any turkey that made it past his or her first year to keep his or her beak shut, or end up as an entrée on the canine menu.

But in breeding season, almost every tom, sooner or later, is going to gobble, at least at daybreak, and at least while he's still on the roost, if not when he hits the ground. After a long night of recuperation from his amorous labors, he is checking for the rest of the troops, particularly the girls, and he is letting the hens know where he is.

I listened to this sound a dozen times in the next half hour and my heart raced faster each and every time. What is it about the way this raucous cry of untamed exuberance falls on the human ear and penetrates the soul? The gobble of a wild turkey has been described by many hunters and outdoor writers as thunderous or booming, as in, "I yelped three times and the gobbler thundered back." Or, "His thunderous gobbles shook the ground." No, they don't shake the ground. They shake the anachronistic caveman of your hunter's heart.

Sometimes a gobble is described as a rattle, as in: "His fierce rattle echoed down through the hollow." To me it is closer to a rattle than to a boom or a thunderclap, but none of these words describes it accurately. The trouble is, I can't figure out which words of the King's English *would* describe it accurately.

It is, to me, an electrifying and almost spectral sound, a kind of terrestrial version of the cry of a loon in terms of the effect it has on the human spirit and psyche. The gobble of a tom turkey not only thrills us and reassures us with its message of wild freedom, but it also stirs in us predatory instincts that are as old as man's presence on earth.

A gobble can startle you if it comes unexpectedly out of nowhere and is very close. If you have hunted hard and not heard this sound much on a particular hunt, an abrupt, unexpected gobble is also an auditory form of manna from heaven. It's like a gift from Santa Claus or the tooth fairy, or your numbers tumbling into the lottery slot. You have just been handed a reprieve. What you do with it is up to you, and to the gobbler, and to how skilled you are at interpreting and reacting to the signals the gobbler sends. For whatever it turns out to be worth, you are one up on the turkeys— you now know where one of them is.

No matter what happens, the gobble of the wild turkey, this wonderful, primitive sound so unlike what most Americans know from hearing the mindless noises in a barnyard or a commercial turkey pen, is one of the main elements in this great sport that keeps us coming back.

Most hunters, even those who have killed a lot of turkeys over a lot of years, consider just hearing a gobble to be the mark of a rewarding day in turkey woods. There is a popular and, I think, valid theory that in many areas today there is less gobbling because generations of toms have absorbed the lesson that being too vocal tips off their position to predators, both human and otherwise. This is the turkey hunter's equivalent of the pheasant hunter's theory that pheasants have genetically adapted down through generations to be runners, not fliers. They are a hell of a lot safer when running through cover than they are while flying through the air. And turkeys are a hell of a lot safer when they're silent than when they sound off.

But when a turkey does gobble, the bird doesn't necessarily have to be called in and killed for the memory of the sound to endure; and so it was this day in western Oklahoma. The Rio Grande gobblers I was hearing turned out to be surrounded by roosted, yelping hens, and when the wildfowl party convened on the ground, the participants pretty much shut up, got down to serious social contact, and had absolutely no interest in moving over to check out a loud, goofy party crasher that was out of sight behind a knoll. They took the party, a very moveable feast, in another direction. My pleading hen yelps went unanswered. I never did catch up, and I was left to contemplate what it is about a hunting sport that can both make a fool out of you and clamp a hammerlock on your determination to keep returning, no matter what.

Besides the sound of the gobble, what *does* keep us coming back? What is it about this peculiar form of outdoor sport that makes it so much different from a dozen or more other types of hunting that lure men, women, and youngsters into the marshes, the river bottoms, the upland coverts, the hills, the mountains, the fields?

First of all, its most rewarding offshoot—spring-season gobbler hunting—takes place at a time of year when there is no other significant form of hunting to be enjoyed. It is a beautiful time of year, a time of awakening and renewal, of impending fulfillment. Mother Earth is coming back to life, increment by increment, sound by sound, color by color, movement by movement. Winter has been defeated again, and you are part of the victory. Just seeing this and hearing this is one of the great joys of turkey hunting.

But I believe that the chief cerebral compulsion can be likened to the fascination of many people for chess, or perhaps bridge. Turkey hunting is a study in strategy, a puzzle of possible moves and countermoves. Turkey hunting, unlike some other forms of hunting, constantly causes the participant to think.

It does not require a hell of a lot of study and analytical thought, for example, to stand at the corner of a wheat or barley field and ambush doves as they pass by in their flight lines. Concentration, timing, good eyesight, shooting skills honed with the expenditure of thousands of shells, yes. Chess-player planning and shrewdness, no.

On a decoying expedition for ducks or geese, most of the planning and strategy is over by the time the hunters climb into the blind or the pit and wait to see if anything with feathers is interested, or even cruising the area. Calling tactics may come into play, but once the decoys are out it is pretty much up to the ducks or the geese and to the weather. You have either chosen the right morning and the right spot or you haven't; the ducks or the geese are going to fly or they are not; they are going to decoy or they are not.

In turkey hunting, it becomes painfully clear that when you haven't chosen the right spot, you have two options: You can either go back to camp or home and hunt again some other time, or you can move. Maybe not far, maybe not more than 200 yards, but you move. Then you may have to move again. And again. If you don't see or hear turkeys, you must determine by the observations you are now making, and already have made in recent days, whether in fact they are just not using the area.

If you move and you finally see or hear a gobbler, you must calculate how far away he is; what he is likely to do if you call from where you are now; whether he has hens with him; whether there is brush, water, a road, or some other obstacle he isn't likely to cross; whether you need to get closer; how best to hide—and you have to make all these and a whole bunch of other decisions that eventually will determine whether you and this gobbler are going to come to know each other on intimate terms, or, in other words, whether you will make your fingers weary plucking feathers. Not only do you have to make all of these choices, but you have to make them fast.

Just as there are very fine chess players, there are people who seem to have a natural knack for playing this gobbler game. They don't start out as expert turkey hunters, but they get that way in relatively short spans of time (a few years is a short span of time in that portion of a hunter's life spent chasing turkeys). They trust what they see and what they hear in the woods. They know how to interpret it. They know that a gobbler they have worked unsuccessfully on a given morning, a bird that appears so old, so big, and so wise as to be almost laughing at their efforts, is a bird that will be vulnerable and foolable on another morning, in another situation. They do their damnedest to create that situation or at least to respond correctly to it when it presents itself spontaneously. These are the kinds of turkeys that make the game infinitely more interesting—and it is already plenty interesting enough.

The finest turkey hunters guess right. Perhaps "guess" is the wrong word, because the guesses they make on what a gobbler will or won't do and when he will do it are based on knowledge, experience, and observation.

The finest turkey hunters are patient, but they aren't immobile or slothful. There is a school of thought that holds that if a gobbler hears you calling, sooner or later he will come to your spot. But a really good turkey hunter isn't inclined to sit there all day and put the theory to the test until the gobbler shows up, night falls, or legal hunting hours come to an end for the day. He will either figure out a different way to approach a hung-up gobbler, or he will find another gobbler. And his brain is always clicking, the wheels are always turning. This is why he is out there. This is why he goes to the trouble of setting all this up. He loves it.

I have always felt, too, that one of the fascinations of this game is the walk to the calling spot in the darkness before dawn. The coming day is full of promise. A game plan has been drafted, and though it may have to be changed almost before it ever begins to be acted out, it is always a good plan until proven otherwise. The night creatures are still out and still vocal—the owls and the whippoorwills, the chuck-will's-widows or the howling coyotes, the snorting, stomping deer, or whatever is native to that particular slice of the turkey's world.

I suppose this is childish, but there is a delicious thrill of adventure and even some degree of risk in traveling on foot through rough country in the dark, a feeling that must be intimately familiar to reconnaissance men engaged in guerilla warfare. You are there, but the idea is not to let the quarry know that you are.

There is the awe and pleasure of watching the wild world come alive for the day, with all the wake-up sounds and tentative, exploratory stirrings that come with it. A chorus of birdsong gradually tunes itself up to a wacky, unconducted symphony of warbles, whistles, chirps, caws, and coos. The early sunlight is as soft as it ever gets, even on the clearest of mornings, and you couldn't feel much more enthralled if you were Dorothy and you and Toto had just touched down in the Land of Oz.

Then there is the breathless, palpable moment when it all comes together: You have done something right, or several things right, and the turkey is coming to your calls. You see him appearing and reappearing through the grass or the brush or the deadfalls or the trees. He is both an apparition and an affirmation, a reassurance, a confirmation that this one thing, at least, is still right with the world. He often comes in with a mincing, measured pace, gobbling and tail-fanning when he stops, then moving again, slowly, almost fragilely (turkeys are living illustrations of the phrase "walking on eggshells"), as if he is not at all positive that what he is hearing is what he hopes it is.

After all, he knows that the hen is supposed to come to him, not vice versa. He has made himself both visible and audible to her and either she is one very dumb broad, or one hard-to-please paramour. Or maybe, his tiny brain tells him, something ain't quite right.

There is an aura around him, a glow. He is the sultan of all he surveys, and his mere presence has made a sultan of sorts out of me when I see him approaching. Wherever and whenever this happens, as I watch him I am more alive than I have been in weeks or months. Every sense I possess is hot-wired and humming, powered by the absolute conviction that this, by God, is what I was really born to do—that I do it only a small percentage of my time on earth makes it all the more captivating and no less valid. The day this doesn't threaten to strangle me with the anticipation and suspense of it all, I'll walk out of the woods and stop hunting turkeys.

Finally, there is the quarry itself. The bird. The gobbler. It is a paradox that a foolish person, or anybody we wish to insult in a good-natured way, is labeled a "turkey." What comes to mind when this word is used in a condescending manner are the sad bunches of domestic turkeys (most of them now pure white) that are crammed pathetically into holding and feeding pens barely with enough room to do anything but stand straight up while they bob their heads and crook their necks and gobble in vacuous repetition, pecking at one another.

The wild turkey is as far from this condition as an eagle is from a chicken. Turkeys, of course, don't fly like eagles; they are reluctant to fly at all, although they can cover a remarkable distance with their noisy, laborious wing beats, followed by a final glide. I once saw a big gobbler fly out of a tall roost tree 150 yards in front of me, continue flying for at least 300 yards, and land atop a rimrock mesa—all just about 20 yards above shotgun range. He knew exactly where I was, had known it since dawn (I must have moved just a hair too much at some point), and if this tom had had a nose, he would have been thumbing it at me.

Gobblers have been decribed as "smart," "wily," and "clever." I am not at all sure that any of those words fit. What a gobbler is, more precisely, is wary and absolutely attuned, virtually at all times, to his environment. After all, something or someone has been trying to kill him and eat him ever since he was hatched out of his shell.

The old bromide about turkey hunting is that "if gobblers could smell, we'd never kill one." More to the point is this: If they didn't breed, we might never kill one, at least not a mature tom in the spring, when birds are scattered. Not just because there wouldn't be any new generations of turkeys coming along for us to hunt, but because there wouldn't be a time when the gobbler had something on his mind besides sustenance and survival. In the fall, we may be able to bust up a flock and call in the scattered young gobblers so easily that it almost seems larcenous. But spring is the only season when the daily distraction of mating gives us an edge over a mature wild creature that at times makes a white-tailed deer seem positively naive.

Then there is the beauty of the bird. Even the dun brown color of a wild hen turkey is beautiful in its subtle way. But during the breeding season the gobbler takes on the iridescence of burnished, polished forms of exotic metal: bronze, black, blue, red, white, gold, brown, buff, gray—they are all there. He may look a little on the preposterous side when he marches stiffly around with his tail feathers spread and his body feathers puffed up, wing tips dragging the ground, emitting that strange drumming sound, or "pulmonic puff." But he is sure as hell impressive. When he isn't strutting, he moves through the trees and the brush and the grass with the grace and coordinated gait of a gazelle, and his form is appealing to the eye.

Which of the four main North American subspecies is the most beautiful? That is a debate that will be worked over in countless hunting camps, lodges, living rooms, bars, and assorted other places for as long as humans hunt turkeys. My view is that the prototype turkey is the Eastern turkey (*Meleagris gallopavo silvestris*); the most exotically colored one is the Rio Grande (*M. g. intermedia*) of the southwestern states; the most streamlined in his long-legged way is the Florida or Osceola turkey (*M. g. osceola*); and the one that looks the biggest and boldest from a distance, partly because of his glaring white-feathered rump, is the Merriam's (*M. g. merriami*), the turkey of the Rocky Mountain West.

I love them all, although I have had less experience with Easterns and Osceolas than with the other two. Most of all, I love the way they make me feel, and make me think.

And I don't even play chess.

2

FIRST TURKEY

I BELIEVE THAT MOST OF US on the downhill side of forty, if overcome with a fit of honesty, would admit that one of the distressing aspects of getting older is that our list of things we remain passionate about has a tendency to get progressively shorter.

In late middle age, a man (assuming he has matured mentally and emotionally as well as physically) is no longer likely to hang out in rock-music nightclubs. If nothing else, he values his hearing too much. Or in poolrooms. Or bars with loud-sound-effect video games. He may have given up on water skiing, cigarette smoking, social marijuana use, subscriptions to *Playboy* magazine, push-powered lawn mowers, motorcycles, sandlot football, jalapeño peppers, convertible cars, and watching late-night talk shows on television. He no longer feels all that strongly about whether the Cubs ever win the pennant or whether he misses a rerun on television of John Wayne in *The Quiet Man*. He has already seen it eleven times.

If he's a hunter or fisherman, some forms of the outdoor sports that got his blood perking when he (or she; let us not lapse totally into male chauvinism) was younger can be filed neatly away now in the I-can-take-it-or-leave-it basket. Like, for instance, hunting ptarmigan at 11,000 feet, or snipe in a willow bog.

Part of this has to do with a common characteristic of the aging process: a diminishing capacity for hard labor, suffering, pretense, self-delusion, hyperbole, and bullshit. If a variation of outdoor sport doesn't measure up, for whatever reasons, to an individual's evolving sense of realizable challenge, comfort level, and fulfillment, no amount of sugarcoating, chastising, or enthusiasm from friends, relatives, or acquaintances can make it otherwise. "You quit hunting elk? What's the matter, man, can't take those timberline hikes anymore?"

To these chidings it does no good to try to explain that what it all amounts to is a clearer vision of one's limitations and the things that really matter personally. We quietly shrug away these impertinent probings, while the list of our tried-and-true passionate pursuits continues to be trimmed down to what still works for us and always will work. Meanwhile, the list of new ones grows so slowly as to become almost stagnant.

So when a man in advanced middle age discovers a new passion, one that he almost immediately senses he will carry with him all the way to the graveyard, however long that journey turns out to be, it is cause for wonderment and rejoicing. It rapidly rises to the level of obsession. Viewed objectively by a nonparticipant from a distance, it may even appear to be a relatively harmless form of madness. But what a fine madness it is to those who are afflicted.

Thus it was for me with turkey hunting. It may be that the joys we discover relatively late in life are the most rewarding of all, if for no other reason than that there are too few of them. And because we wonder why the hell it took us so long.

As a full-time outdoor writer, I was at least obliquely aware of the fact that steadily growing numbers of American hunters in all regions of the country were pursuing turkeys in either spring or fall or both, and that wild turkey populations had made an astounding rebound from the dismal times that extended from the last part of the nineteenth century through the first half of the twentieth century.

But having grown up in east Texas—which, until some relatively recent Eastern subspecies transplanting programs, was a section of that otherwise turkey-rich state that was devoid of turkeys—and having moved to a western state (Colorado) that has limited numbers of turkeys because of limited habitat, I deftly deposited spring turkey hunting into the folder labled "Things to Do Someday."

Then I met Doug Harbour. Doug, of Lamar, in southeastern Colorado, is the son of the late Dave Harbour, a World War II fighter pilot who spent his first career as an officer in the air force, and his later, outdoor-writing career as "Col. Dave Harbour."

The Colonel wrote a wealth of magazine pieces (many for *Sports Afield*) about turkey hunting. Then he took his obsession a step further, authoring two books on turkey hunting, *Hunting the American Wild Turkey* and *Advanced Wild Turkey Hunting and World Records,* the latter in cooperation with the National Wild Turkey Federation.

The colonel taught his son well. Sniffing out a story, I looked up Doug at a sportsmen's exposition one winter in Denver, where he was giving seminars on spring gobbler hunting. I did a feature newspaper piece on Doug's exploits, tips, and expertise as a turkey hunter and guide.

"Come on down to my end of the state and hunt with me this spring," he said. "You might like it."

And martians may land on the White House lawn, I thought some several weeks later as I tossed, turned, and stuffed toilet paper into my ears while trying fitfully to get to sleep in a small camping trailer parked along a creek bottom in the rugged canyon breaks of southeastern Colorado. My trailermate, a man from Pennsylvania who must have weighed 230 pounds despite being only slightly taller than your average golf bag, lay on his back in the upper bunk and bellowed out snores reminiscent of a Hereford bull in a cowless cow pasture.

This man, I had learned, was on a mission: He was determined this particular spring to bag the "Grand Slam." He had taken an Osceola turkey in Florida and an Eastern in some other state, and now all that stood between him and the Holy Grail of all four U. S. turkey subspecies were a Merriam's (which is what this juniper-dotted, creek-carved canyon held) and a Rio Grande, which he would seek shortly thereafter in another state.

We got off to a tardy start at dawn the next day, thanks to a cranky alarm clock, and God, was I happy about that. The difference between struggling out of a sleeping bag at 5:00 A.M. as opposed to 3:45 A.M. may sound like splitting somnolent hairs, but not to a guy who has been buffeted with bull-alligator grunts from his roommate for hours the night before.

"We're late," yelled Doug, splashing hot water into cups laced with instant coffee granules and glancing alternately at his watch and the eastern sky. He was bunked under the tin-roof protection of an old abandoned mining shed near the trailer, where the loudest sleep destroyers were mice skittering around on the concrete floor. I made a mental note to request a transfer to the mouse house.

Late? Stars still winked in the dark-gray western half of the sky, but I had a half-remembered understanding that spring turkey hunting somehow was linked to being a sunrise voyeur, preferably from a position chosen the night before and reached well in advance of the first silver tints on the eastern horizon.

Some minutes later I was riding in the cab of a pickup truck with Doug as he whipped the vehicle around bends in the dirt road, hell-bent for some spot along another cottonwood-lined creek bottom. Pennsylvania's Grand Slam snorer and another hunter in our camp would hunt in nearby areas.

Doug pulled off the road abruptly and parked the truck in a stand of scrub oak. We gathered shotgun and turkey-calling devices (Doug had the callers and I had the gun, since my experience at the time was confined to the latter implement), and we hurriedly sneaked along the creek toward the roost trees.

It was almost full daylight when we plopped down behind a deadfall cottonwood log, I with a 12 gauge over-under, choked full and modified and loaded with No. 4 shot, and Doug with what looked like a latex-covered miniature plastic horseshoe that he snugged into his mouth. He gummed it like an old geezer trying to reposition his dentures. Then he made noises come out of it. They sounded to me like the plaintive yelps of a lost puppy (were we hunting cocker spaniels?). But the turkeys in the aged, angular cottonwoods around the creek bend loved it. They cut loose with a cacophony of answering yelps mixed with virulent gobbles from the male birds.

I listened in awe to these wild noises. Until then, I had thought that the wildest sounds in the outdoors were the honking of Canada geese, the cry of a loon, and the bugle of a rutting elk. I looked at the western landscape brilliant with the first rays of sunlight on a spring morning, the deep chartreuse greens of the budding trees backed by the rust-colored sandstone and the limestone cliffs of the rim of the shallow canyon. And at that moment I knew that I had wasted far too many years, years in which I did not hear the ghostly go-to-hell response of a tom gobbling back at a barred owl in the predawn darkness of wild-turkey country; years in which I did not witness the slanting rays of a rising sun backlighting the tail feathers of a strutting gobbler that looks as big as a Volkswagen.

What I didn't know at the time was that in turkey-hunting terms, we were in trouble. Doug frowned. "Lots of hens," he muttered.

Hens, as I would come to learn, are the single biggest obstacle looming between an early-morning turkey hunter and his hopes of bagging a gobbler. Call in the hen or hens, and you have a damned good chance at the tagalong gobbler; other than that it's a crapshoot with the dice loaded against you.

Ignorance, though, is bliss. Blissfully, I crouched behind the log and strained to look through the juniper trees and assorted brush that broke up the uneven terrain between us and the roost trees. Then there was a clear, high-pitched, sort of chopped-up gobble, more muffled now because it came from the ground instead of the trees. It sent a shiver through me. My knees quaked, whether from the sound or from the sharp bite of the early-morning chill, I wasn't sure.

"Choo-choo gobbler," whispered Doug.

I learned later that this was his way of telling me a jake was on the way in. This tom's juvenile gobbles were impressive until they dissolved intermittently into adolescent clucks. But this bird had the fire of pubescent youth and he could fan his tail and he could strut. Now I could see him, pausing in his deliberate but steady forward progress to stretch out his neck and gobble, just behind the nervous-looking hen he was trailing. His white-fringed tail feathers spread in an impressive imitation of one of the big boys. He looked plenty grown-up to me.

The two birds, still circling to the right, were momentarily lost from sight through the trees and brush, and I concentrated on remembering that before I shot I was supposed to look for, one, the red head and neck of a gobbler, and two, the beard of a gobbler.

The red head appeared again in a small opening to our right, and I saw the stubby, bushy appendange from the upper front of the bird. He still trailed the hen, who was looking more and more edgy, walking faster and swinging farther and farther to our right and to our rear. "I can shoot him when he clears that tree," I whispered to Doug. "Okay," was all he whispered back. What I remember most about my mentor and partner at that moment was that he had not so much as turned his head, not to mention his body. He seemed to be staring straight ahead, where the birds no longer were. But if eyeballs actually clicked, I'm sure his, straining to look to the right, would have sounded like agates banging together in a kid's marble game.

Observing this paragon of immobility may have been the reason I had the presence of mind to move very, very slowly, turning just enough to my right side to bead down on the young tom when he appeared in the little clearing 30 yards to our right. It helped immensely that I was a left-handed shooter. A right-handed shooter in that situation would have had to do almost a 180-degree turnaround and might well have spooked the birds.

I aimed for the red neck–red head junction and pulled the trigger. The walking turkey went down and the gray-headed hen in front of him stopped, looked back, and then ran out of sight.

"Damn fine gobbler," Doug said minutes later. There had been no need for a second shot. The plump bird, as we later determined, weighed 15 pounds. Its beard was 4 inches long.

"But just a jake," I said, already practicing up to sound like a veteran gobbler chaser.

Doug gave me a slight shake of the head and a frown that changed into a sly grin. "You'll learn," he said, tossing the iridescently feathered tom into the bed of the truck, "that any gobbler is a good gobbler."

And so I did, eventually. The temptation then was to conclude that this spring turkey-hunting proposition might not be the ruggedly arcane, existentially tough challenge it was cracked up to be. After all, here I was, a late sleeper (better late than never) fifteen minutes into his first turkey hunt, and I was tagging a gobbler.

Still, however easy this game might be, the desired object of it, I thought, staring at the bronzes, blacks, and whites of the jake's feathered armor, was undoubtedly the Bird of Paradise. I had never seen anything with feathers that looked quite so beautiful to me.

My ego puffed up like a drumming tom when the guy from Pennsylvania, who had not scored this particular morning, later said, "Nice jake. Real nice jake. Good job." He said it almost wistfully, as if he might come to the end of this hunt and wish he had killed the bird. Or maybe he was recalling his own first turkey.

Bird of Paradise, indeed. But I would come, in future years, in future springs, in turkey country from South Florida to Missouri to Kansas to Wyoming, to understand one thing quite clearly: Bird of Purgatory often was a more apt description. Because, you see, there is almost always a degree of penance to undergo before arriving at the Pearly Gates. And I would become truly an expert, if not on killing turkeys, then at least on the levels of suffering that either lead to that heavenly portal or deposit the weary traveler into a gobblerless ditch along the way.

3

SOLO FLIGHT

I HIKED AS QUIETLY AS I COULD up the base of the rocky, juniper-dotted slope and searched for a reasonably comfortable and tactically feasible place to sit and call, a spot that would let me and my gun command a relatively flat, open patch of grass with scattered small bushes at the bottom of the slope, where I hoped a gobbler would appear.

On the slope there were two small juniper trees close together with a shadowy spot between their almost-touching branches. I nestled back in the branches and cleared a few rocks away from the loose dirt under my hips. I estimated the distance down to the flat

23

below me at about 30 yards. Ten yards beyond that was what was left of a dilapidated barbed-wire fence strung parallel to the base of the ridge. Anything on the far side of the fence would be out of sure shotgun range.

This place, chosen the evening before, would be a gamble. There was no more than a 30-yard-wide area out in front where a shot was possible, and no more than 10 yards of depth, unless the gobbler did a 90-degree turn and came straight uphill through rocks and brush to my position, which was unlikely. But any gobbler headed west along the creek valley floor to get to the open draw behind and to the left of me, which was a regularly used turkey route to the mesa rim, would likely cross this small clearing.

I unbuckled my camo fanny pack, sat it beside me and unzipped it, and pulled up the camo face mask dangling around my neck. I shivered in the predawn chill of this early May morning in southern Colorado's mesa country. The ingenuously clear, starlit sky was beginning to be pewter-colored to the east, above the shadowy rim of the shallow canyon. There was only the smallest hint of a breeze.

Downhill from me a few hundred yards, a tea-colored creek coursed along undercut banks partially eroded by decades of stock grazing. The creek and its tiny tributaries and open draws had carved out a rocky canyon on the southern perimeter of the plains of eastern Colorado. Brooding, dark mesas dominated the horizon to the west, toward the foothills of the Rocky Mountains. The canyon, seen from the air, appears as a dark green handprint on the sere tan facade of the arid plains. To the east stretch unfathomable miles of mostly flat ground checkerboarded with grassland plots and wheat fields. A first-time visitor driving across those flats to this little canyon is surprised to see it suddenly appear, sprawled out below him, the first geological and topographical hint of those distant "shining mountains" of Ute tribal lore.

I was enveloped in the wonderful, unique flavor of western turkey country. A pack of coyotes sounded off far behind me, somewhere on the mesa top, probably celebrating the capture of one or more cottontail rabbits of the kind I was now seeing bounding from grass clumps to bushy cover down on the flat in front of me. Several hundred yards to my west a Hereford bull let out a bellow-moan as if to express his disgust that he was still fenced inside a pasture without a single nubile heifer in sight. The last late-night shift of barred owls was sending out its farewell salute to the dwindling darkness.

It seemed a perfect morning for a repeat of the chorus of gobbling I had heard down along the creek the evening before.

As if to second the motion, two roosted gobblers on the cottonwood-lined creek bottom, out of sight to my right, began to rattle their greetings to the dawn even before I could bring the owl hooter to my lips. I smiled to myself, wondering why I would need to sound like an owl when several of the real thing were already singing. I slipped the hooter back into the hip pack and extracted my cedar box caller, laid it aside, then reached into a shirt pocket for a snap-lid plastic box that contained two diaphragm callers, one a double-reed Boss Hen with a raspy sound and the other a Kee Kee diaphragm with a high-pitched yelp. The only reason I had included it was that it had a more pliable reed than the Boss Hen, and I had been having trouble using the stiffer double reed.

I had spent the idle hours of an entire fall and winter practicing on both the box and the diaphragms, with mixed results. One of the results was that both the dog and my wife found sudden compelling reasons to go out in the backyard, or go for a drive, or go down to the basement.

Another result, for the first few weeks or so, was the onset of periodic spasms of gagging. My gag reflex has always been superb, and it didn't let me down when I first began stuffing a half-moon-shaped yelper into my mouth (I had enough sense to position the open end outward, but for a while that's about all I did right).

After reading a turkey-hunting story in which a box-caller expert advised stroking the box paddle with a loose, limp wrist movement, I found that my loose-wristed box yelps became more or less passable, or at least they sounded like what I was hearing on my instructional tape. And I finally got to where I could yelp a bit with the diaphragms, particularly the single reed, although I suspected that my tongue technique (sorry, but that's the best way I can describe it) was something less than standard operating procedure. Or something more, maybe. The feeling was that I was forcing something I didn't need to force, and as I found out in later years, it doesn't take gale-strength exhalations to make a sound come out of a piece of stretched latex.

The light grew and it was time to call. The gobblers were periodically doing what they are supposed to do—gobble—and there were some answering hen yelps from farther down the creek to the east. I had better let one or more of these toms know where I was with some believable hen sounds or I was going to lose all of them to the real thing.

Involuntarily I shivered again, not entirely from the cold. My left knee seemed to have a motor of its own, vibrating uncontrollably. I now understood fully, if I hadn't earlier, why spring turkey hunting is essentially a solitary sport. You do not need somebody else there to get you fired up about the whole affair, and there is a sense of adventure in knowing that whatever happens, the only person who is going to influence its outcome is you.

I was hunting in only my second spring season, and I had been looking forward to it, dreaming about it, for months. I had killed a jake gobbler the year before in the company of my friend Doug Harbour, a highly experienced and crafty turkey hunter who was at this moment carrying out his own calling ambush somewhere at the west end of the canyon. We had set up camp together, but he had advised me strongly to hunt on my own.

"It's time," he said in that mischievous way of his with the characteristic crooked Harbour grin, "you became a big boy. Time to graduate."

It was solo time, in other words. And somehow, for some reason, based on no more than one short hunt the year before and the eager reading of two books on the subject, this little challenge meant more to me than almost any comparable moment I had experienced in a lifetime of pursuing deer, elk, ducks, geese, pheasants, antelope, and a long list of other wild creatures that walk or fly the earth.

We had arrived in the area about midafternoon the day before. I had spent the rest of the afternoon hunting the wide draw that led down to the winding creek, changing positions periodically and hoping to call in a tom that might be migrating downhill from the mesa top to the creekside roost trees. I neither heard nor saw a turkey.

But shortly after the sun set, I discovered, when I reached the creek and hop-skipped across the shallow ford to reach my parked vehicle on the other side, that several turkeys had walked down off the mesa and ended up in the cottonwoods along the creek. They had gone to roost without me seeing a single one of them.

I learned this when, on a whim, as the soft shadows of dusk settled over the little valley, I did my best imitation of a gobble call just to see if it stirred any response. Since I didn't know how to gobble with my box caller and I didn't have a tube shaker, I improvised. In a burst of inspiration, I fake-gobbled by sticking the Kee Kee diaphragm in my mouth, blowing hard across its reed, and sticking my right index finger in my mouth at the same time. Simultaneously while huffing and puffing outward I jiggled the finger, causing my lips to break up the sound, and thereby making a noise that I hoped sounded like a turkey gobbling.

It was good enough to raise the hackles of three gobblers down the creek to the east. They gobbled back. Encouraged by this, I noted what I figured were their approximate locations (for purposes of positioning myself the following morning). That night, Doug would suggest the slope overlooking the fence-line flat.

Emboldened by my success with the finger routine, I took both the finger and the diaphragm out of my mouth and cut loose with what can only be described as a totally existential, off-the-wall, spontaneous voice-call-only gobble. Not knowing how else to do it, I yelled, in my best fake falsetto, "Gobble, gobble, gobble." Or syllables to that effect.

To my amazement and delight, the three gobblers, joined by one more in the same area, answered right back.

Not bad for the takeoff of a solo flight. I had roosted four gobblers for the morning hunt.

Now, in the gathering light of a new day, listening to at least two of the same four toms as they were about to leave their roost limbs and go about their morning's business, I had a choice to make: mouth diaphragm or box caller?

I stuck the Boss Hen yelper in my mouth and huffed away. And got what sounded like a parrot choking on a piece of popcorn. Shades of my gagging days. I panicked. Funny thing: You can produce the finest-sounding turkey yelps any trained ear could imagine in, as they say, "the comfort of your own home," but take that act to the real woods and find yourself in the presence of a real gobbler, and suddenly there is something wrong with your throat. (These pesky viruses are everywhere and crop up at the worst times.)

I put the mouth yelper away and reached for the box. I chalked it one final time, then stroked out four yelps in what I hoped was a rhythmic, believable sequence.

The closest tom, maybe 200 yards to my right but well out of sight past the contours and trees of the ridge I was on, cut off the last yelp with a ferocious gobble.

Aw right! So far, so good. My knees settled down to idling speed.

I worked the box at five-minute intervals. The next time the tom gobbled, it sounded as if he was farther away. I hurriedly stroked out more yelps, and he answered again. I had a mental picture of him wandering in the opposite direction toward the distant hens I had heard earlier and nervously produced another sequence of yelps on the box.

No answer. I pondered this. I tried to think in terms of an experienced turkey hunter, which I resembled in outward appearance only. Then a couple of things occurred to me that Doug had said earlier: "After they fly down, they always sound farther away when they gobble on the ground. That's because the contours of the terrain, the tree and brush cover, muffle the sound that you were hearing earlier when the bird was in the tree." And, "If a gobbler shuts up after at first answering your calls, it doesn't necessarily mean he's lost interest. He may be on his way to you, and he may not gobble again until he gets there."

Minutes passed in the plodding pace of the passage of eons. I got more and more antsy. The temptation was strong to pick up the box and use it again. I was about to succumb to the pressure and had just grabbed the box handle when one more thought occurred: There was only a narrow corridor of open ground down on the flat in front of me and any gobbler that came to my calls would be in gun range at the same instant I saw him.

Right now, he could be no more than 50 yards away, out of sight to my right (or left), and if he didn't gobble I wouldn't know it until he stepped out onto the green grass of that flat stage below me. Loud yelps at 50 yards might serve more to alert the gobbler than to draw him closer. I held back on the box.

And then, in my right-hand peripheral vision a shape appeared, the dark, walking, mincing shape of a turkey. He, or she, was walking from my right to my left along the barbed-wire fence line, on my side of the fence. The range was already inside 40 yards, and a few more steps would put the bird square in front of and below me at no more than 30 yards.

My first reaction was to wonder whether this was a hen or a tom. Since my turkey-watching exerience was limited, and since I had no other turkey or turkeys around to compare this bird to in terms of size, I really had no clue, even though this looked like a large bird. I briefly imagined myself walking down to claim my just-shot turkey and finding to my horror that it was a hen.

There was a small bush in front of the turkey, and when the bird walked between the bush and the fence, I brought the gun up to firing position. If it was a gobbler, I would be ready.

The bird stopped, for some reason, behind the bush. I had not yet seen a beard, and the early morning light was still too flat for me to make out the red, white, or blue of a gobbler's head and neck. I remembered the stories I had read of gobblers possessed of some extrasensory perception who stopped behind bushes or tree trunks and then for no apparent reason ran straight away from the hunter, keeping the bush or tree in the line of fire.

I concentrated on putting the little bead on the front end of the shotgun barrel just to the left of the bush, and on keeping my head down on the stock.

The turkey silently, gracefully, walked out on the left side of the bush. The bird moved as if negotiating hot coals or a minefield, one hesitant step at a time. Early sunlight bounced off the budding yellowish green grass between the bush and the fence, and, framed against this lighter backdrop, I saw a sparse but fairly long beard sticking out in front of the juncture of breast and neck. As the gobbler took another step the beard swung outward a bit. I beaded down where the neck met the head and pulled the trigger.

The boom must have sounded shockingly loud in the morning stillness, but I was barely aware of it. The gobbler did a somersault, flopped two or three times, and lay almost still, except for a few reflexive wing beats.

I sat there, frozen, still looking down the barrel. I stood up stiffly, discovered that my left leg had fallen asleep, almost fell back down, then laid the gun side the fanny pack and the box caller. And then I startled myself by yelling at the top of my lungs. Where this came from I am not sure, but eventually, through the years, it would become a sort of habitual personal quirk that, for the most part, nobody knew about but me.

Then I picked up the gun again (nothing would be more foolish, or deflating, than to watch the tom jump up and run away wounded, and me without a gun in my hand) and walked down to examine the second gobbler of my life.

There was no need to worry about a second shot. The tom—he weighed 20 pounds on the camp scale, and he had an 8-inch beard—was still. I knelt beside him and stroked the glowing bronzes and blacks and white rump feathers of a beautiful Merriam's turkey. The bird appeared to be about two years old, maybe three, with blunt spurs worn off short of the inch mark by thousands of encounters with the rocks of this western turkey habitat.

The sun sparkled now through the pastel greens of the budding cottonwoods and the land fairly glowed, as did the man who stood there rather stupidly (if you were observing him from a distance) and stared at the bird, feeling the peculiar twinge of regret that comes momentarily with every kill. I took a cigarette out of a pack I only carry with me now on hunting and fishing trips (I usually end up tossing half the pack away later), lit it, and took a deep drag. Tobacco never tasted better, although in my younger years I had been a pack-a-day smoker. If it always tasted like this I'd be a two-pack-a-day man and a candidate for the cancer ward.

Solo flight complete. Beautiful landing. The sky was mine and the horizons went on forever.

4

BIRD OF PURGATORY

THIS CAN BE AND HAS BEEN DEBATED, but it's my conviction that some people are natural-born turkey hunters and some aren't. It has to do, in large measure, with individual styles, personalities, and the idiosyncrasies of human nature.

Sport-specific above-average talents and abilities aren't confined to turkey hunting, of course. There are some hunters who are relentless, skillful predators of white-tailed deer but who couldn't kill an elk if they had a month to do it in and three or four states to choose from. There are some who are deadly on crossing doves riding a tailwind but who couldn't hit a straight-out-in-front, going-away pheasant if the bird somehow went into fast rewind and gave them two more chances. There are some who can knock a dipping, diving teal stone-cold into the water but can miss a Canada goose gliding into decoys at 25 yards. There are some who can find the single biggest mule deer in a 10-square-mile section of rough terrain but don't have a clue where to begin looking for sharp-tailed grouse.

Understand, there is not a damned thing wrong with being brilliant at one undertaking and average or even below average at something else. And anybody who says there is needs to consider signing up for an ego-shrinking program. There is no etched-in-granite edict that says the turkey hunter who isn't—and probably never will be—instinctively shrewd at it won't kill his share of gobblers. He most assuredly will, if he hangs in there. The important thing is that he loves it and is out there trying. But his share, in the long run, will be smaller than the shares of those who seem, somehow, to be able to think like a gobbler.

All of us, in our myriad ranges of capabilities, are inevitably going to struggle from time to time. Even the guy I know who travels to four or five turkey states every year and bags at least one gobbler in each state and seems to know where a gobbler wants to go even before the bird does has days when he walks back to camp, or drives home, without a turkey.

As mentioned earlier in these musings, the wild turkey is often much closer to being the Bird of Purgatory than the Bird of Paradise. As the *Oxford English Dictionary* defines it, purgatory is "a place or condition in which souls undergo purification by temporary punishment; a state of suffering."

If we apply this axiom to spring turkey hunting, the purest soul I know is my friend Bill Shappell. But anything can be carried to extremes, even soul purging. Though all of us millions of miscreants who love turkey hunting can identify with the days in the woods when we are lost in a netherworld of temporary penance and self-inflicted misfortune, going turkeyless and at times clueless, Bill seems to make a specialty of it.

This, mind you, is the same man who can manage a large tackle shop, down a double on a bobwhite covey flush, fool a 20-inch brown trout on a #22 dry fly and land it on 3-pound test tippet, double-haul a bulky saltwater streamer into a headwind to lead a cruising tarpon 70 feet from the boat, tie an exquisite trout fly, and, not incidentally, mix a hell of a fine Bloody Mary or Manhattan. He is by no means bereft of skills. But for a while there I thought Murphy's Law would become Bill's Law before he walked out of the woods with a gobbler slung over his shoulder.

He absolutely will not shoot a jake, or at least hasn't yet. This, I tried to advise him, might be part of the problem. I asked him once during those trying seasons before he finally nailed a gobbler, if he remembered his first sexual encounter.

"Absolutely," he replied, a fond, faraway look in his eyes.

"Well," I asked, "it wasn't with Marilyn Monroe, was it?"

I am sure he comprehended the point: You have to start everything somewhere. But he was loath to settle for a jake as his first turkey.

Gradually, though, I think he began to change his thinking and adjusted himself to the reasonable proposition that a major journey, even into the realm of successful turkey hunting, must begin with a first step. Not to mention the fact that a year-old gobbler is just about as good to eat as a wild fowl ever gets.

Then came the spring when it appeared that Bill's prolonged penance was at an end.

We had just arrived in our southern Colorado hunting area and were setting up camp, which happened to be in a rancher's haystack yard about 100 yards off a gravel county road. There was a two-track rut road used by ranch-hand wranglers leading from the county road to the stack yard and then gradually up the little valley toward the distant roost trees along the canyon-bottom creek to the north of the haystack.

While Bill finished shifting some stuff from the four-wheel-drive vehicle (it happens to be a white Ford Bronco that for months

occasionally drew yells and waves from grinning occupants of passing cars: "Hey, O.J.!"), I unfolded a lawn chair and sat down to take
a break. My gaze drifted toward the distant creek, and I considered
digging out a pair of binoculars to scan the brush and grass alongside the creek to see if any turkeys had wandered out of the trees
for an afternoon feed.

I didn't need binoculars. I blinked in astonishment at what was
obviously a Merriam's gobbler, either a large jake or a two-year-
old with a broomed-off beard, walking casually and steadily down
the rut road toward the two humans, the haystack, the camping
trailer, and the glaring, white vehicle. And he was almost in range.
He seemed not terribly alarmed by this rather conspicuous conglomeration of gear, piled-up cow feed, and humanity. Maybe he
was accustomed to seeing ranch vehicles drive up to the stack and
load hay bales.

We have come to expect the unexpected on a turkey hunt, but
we are not in the habit yet of sitting around camp with loaded guns
in our laps. I whispered to Bill and pointed to the oncoming turkey.

"Are you shitting me?" he said, blinking into the bright afternoon sunshine. No, I assured him, I was not. Then he saw the gobbler, but by the time Bill, in a kind of disbelieving, slow-motion
panic, had retrieved his callers and his shotgun from the vehicle,
the tom had veered off west across a cactus-studded pasture and
was walking hurriedly away, about 30 yards out of range.

Just for the purgatory of it, Bill stuck a diaphragm in his mouth
and hen-yelped three times.

The tom stopped, looked back, and gobbled!

Bill, already clad in camouflage, dropped down into the nearby
creek bottom and began to try to circle ahead of the tom. This
obviously wasn't the brightest bird in the woods, and he could be
called in easily.

Bill now was out of sight, and I fished out the binoculars. As I
settled back in the lawn chair to watch the show, the thought
occurred that all I needed now was a can of beer and some nachos.

I looked through the optics to see the turkey suddenly break into a run. I assumed Bill was now set up and calling, but in the wind I couldn't hear it. Eager gobblers sometimes come to calls on the run. Was I about to have a grandstand view, binocular-assisted, of Bill bagging his first gobbler? Was he about to emerge triumphant from the shadowland into paradise?

Not exactly, as they used to say in the rental-car commercials. We weren't the only predators around who had concluded that this was a less-than-alert turkey.

The tom was running because a very large and very bold ferruginous hawk had dived out of the sky straight for the gobbler's head and neck. The tom fought back, raking with his feet in a kind of backward-flopping posture that looked positively slapstick. The hawk quickly concluded that this turkey dinner, which had to weigh at least three times as much as the hawk, was a bit too big a bite. The hawk flew off and the tom ran full speed again, disappearing into the brush. If all this strains credulity, I understand. It certainly strained mine. If I had seen this sequence on one of those made-for-TV nature shows, I would have assumed it involved trained birds.

Hawk attacks, of course, border on divine intervention in the makings of an unsuccessful hunt. And certainly my friend Bill's stay in turkey purgatory is an extreme case. The other certainty was that someday, with faith and hard hunting, he would ascend from it. And eventually he did. But not without a few more bouts of suffering along the way.

All of us, if we have spent much time in turkey woods, have been where he was, sometimes for hours, sometimes for days, sometimes for most or all of a spring season. It may be a case of adverse weather (quite often it's wind, the curse of the turkey caller). It may just be a temporary localized shortage of turkeys, one of those low years in the cycles of turkey reproduction and over-winter survival. Or it may be our own mistakes: bumping a bird off the roost at dawn, calling too much, hiding inadequately, getting up from hiding too soon, moving too much, moving too little. Then there's the one that none of us likes to talk about or think much about, because it's not supposed to happen: We flat out miss the turkey. At easy range. Standing there like a statue (the turkey, not the hunter).

Which brings us back, alas, to poor Bill. He is aggressive in his outdoor pursuits, which stands him in good stead for some things but not necessarily for others. He is somewhat impatient and fidgety. If something doesn't happen, he wants to make it happen. When hunting turkeys he tends to move too much and hide too little. He is inclined to change hunting areas when a change isn't the answer.

The very next day after the hawk incident, I called in a mature tom as Bill sat beside me in a clump of brush, his gun at the ready. He would be the shooter. This tom was as hot as any turkey I ever heard. But when the tom didn't appear within a few minutes, I had to dissuade Bill from trying to move closer. This bird wanted to come, in the worst way. There were a few obstacles in his path, but we were too damned close to risk shifting positions.

The tom, tail-fanning almost every step of the way, finally came across a deep gulley and around a wall of brush to get to us. He emerged in the little clearing in front of us and stood there, strutting, at exactly 38 yards range. (I stepped the yardage off later.) For many full-choke shotguns, this is within the range at which the pattern spreads to its maximum effectiveness.

My partner fired his load of No. 4s from a comfortable sitting position. The turkey stiffened, stood there, looked straight at us for a moment, and then ran away. Bill was so stunned at not seeing the bird fall that he never fired a second shot. We tracked the escape route of the tom for a while but found nothing to indicate that so much as a feather had been misplaced by a piece of lead shot.

I offered condolences but restrained myself and delivered no lectures. And good gobbler, am I glad! Because I went out the next morning by myself and did precisely the same thing.

This time, a tom was trailing a flock of six hens that had flown down off the roost with him. The little group was feeding along almost exactly in line with the tree under which I was calling. The tom even obligingly wandered off to the side so he wouldn't be standing too close to the hens when it came time to shoot him.

When he was about 35 yards away and coming head-on, I pulled the trigger. Nothing happened, at least nothing that I expected. The tom gobbled at the boom of the gun as if he thought it was a thunderclap. I was so flabbergasted I must have frozen for a second. The hens looked in the direction of the sound, then started running in a panic. Luckily for me, they were confused and didn't know which direction to take or exactly where or what the danger was. Because they were milling uncertainly, so did the tom, and I managed to roll him with a follow-up shot that was more like a rabbit hunt than a turkey ambush.

Purgatory was that close.

There is no doubt in my mind that the pattern from the first shot sailed directly over the gobbler's head. I had casually, confidently, aimed high, at the head (which, when you think about it, is no bigger than a mourning dove). I had not made a conscious, concentrated effort to put the bead of the Beretta on the gobbler's neck, which is insurance against wasting the bottom half of the shot pattern. Then I had looked up off the stock as I fired (the better to watch the bird fall, of course).

No doubt Bill had made the same oversight, literally, the day before. If I made another mistake, it was shooting too soon. Even though the bird was well within range of a full-choke 12 gauge, he was still plodding steadily in my direction. I could have waited until he was 20 or 25 yards away, or presumably until he elected to crawl into my lap.

Realizing our mistakes helps us buy a ticket out of purgatory. It won't be a one-way ticket though, because sooner or later, we will make the same errors again, or variations thereof. That's what makes this obsession called turkey hunting so intriguing.

Footnote: Bill got his gobbler, a mature bird with an 8-inch beard, the next spring about 2 miles from where he missed the one the year before. We were again sitting together, calling, only because both of us happened to be in camp when we heard the tom, presiding over a harem of three hens, gobble from 300 yards away.

As it turned out, I beat Bill to the punch in terms of trying to find a way to screw it all up. The tom came to the raspy sounds of a box caller even though he already had company, but when he swung to our extreme right to avoid walking through a dense wall of dry weeds, I assumed Bill (a right-handed shooter) would be unable to get turned around enough to aim and fire.

Not taking another look at Bill, I fired, left-handed, from marginal range. (What I had failed to see was that Bill had managed to squirm around to the right of his tree trunk and was within two seconds of pulling the trigger himself, and he was 10 yards closer to the bird). At my shot the tom went down. We got up from our cramped positions. But while I stood there prematurely counting coup, the gobbler scrambled back up. I was amazed, caught completely flat-footed and in no position to shoot. Bill calmly, quickly, and deftly brought his gun to his shoulder and anchored the running turkey, which was very swiftly making an exit with no discernible hitch in his stride.

I was already aware that Bill was pretty damned good on going-away pheasants.

Some skills, it would seem, are transferable. And purgatory is just a pothole in the road to paradise.

5

THE JUNIPER

W. SOMERSET MAUGHAM ONCE WROTE, "Sometimes a man hits upon a place to which he mysteriously feels he belongs." Tom Kelly, of southern Alabama, puts it this way: "There is always a half-section of land, somewhere, that fits you better than it does anybody else."

I quote these writers not to demonstrate my eclectic choice of reading material but to make the point that all of us have discovered special places we go back to repeatedly in our outdoor pilgrimages. Some of these places go beyond special: They border on mystical.

One of mine is considerably smaller than a half-section. It is a single juniper tree.

This particular old and gnarly Western juniper, or cedar, as these trees are often called in the West, grows amid a scattered clutter of smaller cedars on a gradual grassy slope leading past a rocky finger ridge and then to a wide draw in some of the best turkey habitat in the state of Colorado. It sprouted decades ago almost on a precise line between the nearest turkey roost trees, ancient cottonwoods along a creek, and the open end of the draw. Turkeys flying down at dawn from the cottonwoods often choose that line to feed uphill into the draw, and from there up and over the rim of a mesa. Once they get up on top, they're scattered in a thick maze of mesatop junipers that make hunting similar to a frustrating exercise in jungle warfare. So the idea is to intercept one before they do.

Western junipers aren't so much trees as they are ragged overgrown bushes, although some can grow as tall as 15 feet. As such, they often don't provide a comfortable trunk for a camouflaged hunter to lean back against, but with their low-level branches they have their own built-in ground-level foliage camouflage.

Because of its age, location, and configuration, this particular juniper not only has a trunk to lean against but is also a perfect hiding place from which to sit and call. The branches part into two handy (but not too wide) openings, allowing a hunter or two to sit back in the shadows and yelp all day, if need be, without suffering the pain and paralysis that come from a root- or rock-filled hideaway. The juniper even sheds a moderate rain shower. The hunter isn't likely to move prematurely for lack of comfort, which is one reason so many gobblers have been called up to it.

Having hunted this area for more than a decade, I know that the juniper has produced more turkeys than any other ten hiding-place trees along the entire creek. The first time I used it, many years ago, I was in a near panic to select a calling spot in the rapidly increasing light of predawn without being spotted by a gobbler sounding off about 150 yards away in the roost-tree cottonwoods.

I peered under the cedar branches. There, half-buried in the soft dirt, was a single empty shot shell, size 4. It was an old and faded shell, but it seemed a good omen. Somebody had fired only one shot, and that usually spells turkey dinner.

The tom gobbled back in response to my soft clucks and, later, to my rendition of a cackle, but he did so with a sort of delayed-reaction timing. He didn't rudely cut off the end of my calls. This told me he was interested, but not necessarily falling all over himself with fiery passion.

I must have been somewhere near what he considered to be the right place, though, because he flew down with a clatter of wings and worked his way in my direction. He stopped about 70 yards downhill, directly in front of the juniper. He listened intently to my calls, cocking his head in a slightly backward position as if critiquing them. But he refused to come a single step closer. After five minutes of this, he walked nonchalantly back in the direction he had come, occasionally gobbling back halfheartedly at my last-ditch attempts to turn him.

Knowing at least one gobbler was in the area, I returned the next morning. I was tempted to set up in the branches of a smaller juniper about 40 yards downhill from the one I had used the day before. But some little voice in my head said, "Stick with what looks like a winner."

Just before the sun peeked over the canyon rim, five hens and a strutting gobbler, maybe the same one but I cannot swear to it, walked straight up to my juniper tree after I offered them two series of yelps on a box caller. The gobbler split away slightly uphill from the hens and did not deviate more than 5 degrees from his head-on bearing toward my hiding place right up to the second I pulled the trigger.

This initial triumph was followed by subsequent successes at the strategic juniper by me and by various hunting partners over the next few years. "In the morning, I think I'll try the juniper over on the other side of the creek ford," came to be understood perfectly, with no geographic embellishment, by anybody in camp. Nevertheless, not all has gone according to turkey-hunting Hoyle from the magic juniper.

Once, as a partner was ferrying me to the spot in his four-wheel-drive pickup, we came bouncing around a little bend and blundered into a drove of turkeys. I have mixed feelings about these unexpected opportunities that involve vehicles. On the one hand, I would give up hunting before I indulged in, or had to depend on, what is commonly called "road hunting." On the other, creeping along a backcountry trail or dirt road in a four-wheel-drive and happening to spot a gobbler, or several turkeys, can be viewed as a stroke of luck. You can either try to take advantage of it or you can go on and forget about it—but there will be enough bad luck in your future that it seems sort of silly not to take advantage of the good kind. Sometimes, on these rare occasions, I have simply decided that I didn't want to take a turkey I didn't call in, and let the gobbler run off.

This particular day, when my partner stopped the truck, I bailed sort of halfheartedly out of the passenger side of the cab with my over-under double and reached into a pocket and jammed a shell in each chamber. But I was too tardy to do much more than wave good-bye to the receding tail feathers of a couple of Merriam's toms.

You see, in Colorado it ain't cricket, nor is it safe or legal, to keep a gun loaded inside a hunting vehicle. So instinctively I cracked open the action, unloaded, and climbed back into the pickup. It seemed pointless to chase after these spooked turkeys and I decided to stick with Plan A: Go to the juniper, a short distance ahead, and set up for an hour or so of afternoon calling (all-day turkey hunting is legal in Colorado).

After being dropped off and crab-scooting back into the juniper branches, I wondered if this was pure folly in view of what had just happened. There could only be so many turkeys within calling distance of the juniper, and the Keystone Kops routine with the truck may have spooked all of them.

Ten minutes later I cut loose with a pretty spiffy run of box-caller yelps and sat back to listen to the cawing crows, the occasional quacks of hen mallards working the creek bottom, and the bawls of grazing cattle several hundred yards away. I did not hear, nor did I expect to hear, a gobble.

Just as I set the box down and looked up, I was amazed to see, about 25 yards to my left, a big gobbler. He had come in silently, as they sometimes do, in answer to my yelps no more than fifteen minutes after the truck fiasco. I was even more amazed—you might say profoundly shocked—when the trigger pull resulted in a metallic click.

When I had gotten out of the truck the second time, I had forgotten to reload. Somewhere there is a psychologist who can explain why one reflexive action (unloading to get back into the truck) somehow supersedes what should be the next reflexive action (reloading upon getting out of the truck again), but all I knew was that I had made a serious mistake. The result of trying to rectify the oversight by fumbling for shells was another set of rapidly receding tail feathers. After that, the juniper and I shared a fine two hours of observing lengthening afternoon shadows, foraging cottontail rabbits, and a pastel sunset.

Then there was the time I and a friend sat in the juniper and grinned as we watched a huge tom fly down from the roost trees. But the tom went the opposite direction, where my son, Slater, was hiding somewhere in the next draw to the east. Twenty minutes later we heard the boom of his gun. Ten minutes after that, as we stood in front of the juniper and waited for him, he emerged from the trees carrying the 23-pound tom over his shoulder.

The juniper hadn't really failed me. It again had been the focal point of another memorable adventure in spring turkey woods. I hardly could be disappointed. This is a cliché that gets used in a variety of semisappy narratives, but I can be just as delighted, in a slightly different way, to witness a successful hunt by a son or close friend as I am to be successful myself.

Slater spent the rest of the day playing the role of younger-gen-
eration camp hero. I have to admit, though, that he kept it modest.
"The gobbler ran straight at me," he marveled. "There wasn't much
way I could screw it up."

At dawn the next day, as my son sat with me under the branches
while I tried to fill my tag, the juniper reminded both of us that all
men, even recently triumphant turkey hunters, are mortal:

Slater, in the half-darkness, sat down smack-dab in the middle
of a fresh cow pie. I can only conclude that a Hereford seeking a
comfortable spot to do its business, and going to the trouble to back
up into the branches of this particular juniper, has exceptional taste
in trees.

6

Two Toms for the Colonel

I HAVE NO IDEA WHAT YOU THINK ABOUT GHOSTS, the spirit world, ectoplasms, seances, or the Hereafter. Most of the time, I don't have a solid idea of what I think about them. But I am convinced that those we have known who have preceded us into whatever awaits us after death can have an influence, almost a presence, in our lives if we let them, or if we are influenced by our memories of them.

All of our personalities and fortunes are partially shaped, in one way or another, by those we know or have known. Or those we revere or admire, whether they are still alive or not, sometimes whether we ever actually met them or not. Boys who grow up to be major league football, baseball, or basketball players, or girls who grow up to be tennis stars, Hollywood actresses, or world-class figure skaters, or whatever destinies call them, often cite—and I have a slight distaste for this term—"role models." Sometimes these are relatives or friends. Sometimes these are people they never met, or met casually once, or simply saw on film, who inspired them. I can think of several words that say it better than role model: fathers, mothers, heroes, teachers, coaches, inspirations, gurus.

The late Dave Harbour was an inspiration, a "role model" if you must, to me. He loved and lived turkey hunting as relatively few others have ever done. It is probably what kept him from dying much sooner than he did from serious heart problems. Known as Col. Dave Harbour, he fought through his health battles and lived long enough to write two books on the skills and fascination of turkey hunting, to become one of the first hunters in the country to bag the Grand Slam of gobblers (all four major subspecies) in a single spring, and with his stories to cast a spell over hunters such as I.

His writing was at times clichéd-sounding, at other times almost flowery, but his stories had the ring of truth, the fervor of dedication and obsession, and the spirit of adventure and human triumph over imposing odds. There was never a doubt about the depth of his love for the sport. He wrote more than once of sitting in hiding at the first silvery hint of dawn, observing the eastern sky go from pewter to gold to blue, listening to the world of turkeys come alive to a new day, and "watching once again that parade of old gobblers go marching by" in his mind. In years to come I was to comprehend exactly what he meant.

Yet I never met the man, though I am close friends with one of his sons, Doug Harbour of Lamar, Colorado. Dave and I talked on the phone a time or two, mostly about conservation issues, and he signed one of his books for me and mailed it to me, but we never hunted together or so much as shook hands. I read those books over and over, until the jacket covers fell away in tatters.

I felt a sense of sadness and loss when Doug called to say that his father had died of a heart attack. But when I learned the circumstances of the death, I couldn't help but feel that Dave had written the script for his own passing.

It happened on a Kansas turkey hunt, a father-son excursion with a couple of other hunters along. The Colonel, who, after having his fighter plane shot out from under him, once stood on a Hawaiian airfield and fired a handgun at strafing Japanese airplanes during the Pearl Harbor attack, was now sixty-eight years old. He was excited about this hunt, and the fever still burned in his eyes when one of the hunters in the party picked him up in the early morning hours at the small-town motel to leave for the hunting area.

The other hunter, Carroll Lange, a biologist with the Kansas state wildlife agency, marveled later: "I have picked up a lot of hunters over the years at that motel, but he was the only one who was standing outside at the curb when I got there." Lange dropped Dave off at his preselected spot, leaving him with his gun and callers and his camp stool to ease his aching bones and aging muscles. As the morning progressed, Lange could faintly hear the Colonel sending out a series of hen yelps. The calling went on for a considerable time, and it was assumed that Dave was carrying out one of his favorite rituals: calling a gobbler into range, then keeping the bird there with teasing yelps and purrs just to revel in the spectacle of the gobbling and strutting and fanning.

Eventually, there was a gunshot from the Colonel's position, then another. Lange went to check on Dave. He found him standing at the bottom of a steep creek bank, looking for the gobbler he had shot. The tom was hard hit, but it had managed to run off.

As was his habit, Dave had marked the bird's direction of flight with white tissue-paper markers stuck to trees and bushes. This made it easier to find the turkey, which was found floating in the creek. (Dave often also used tissue or toilet paper to mark his way out of a circuitous obstacle-laden path back to camp after roosting a tom at nightfall, the better to retrace his steps in the morning.)

As the Colonel and his companion bent to admire and tag the big Rio Grande gobbler, Dave remarked that it was the most beautiful tom he could ever remember taking—and that included a lot of gobblers.

Just then he settled slowly to the ground and said something like, "I'd better rest a second." And within moments, he died.

Two weeks later, Doug Harbour, after attending to his father's funeral, decided the best thing he could do in his grief-numbed state was to go ahead and go on the turkey hunt the two of us had planned in Colorado. So I met him there, and we sat in our makeshift camp building, an old, abandoned, dilapidated mine-processing shed, and lifted a few to the Colonel.

Two other hunters from out of state were in camp according to long-prior arrangements, and Doug was acting as their sort of unpaid guide. They were a husband-and-wife team and they bunked in a nearby trailer.

The wife was well versed in the basics of most forms of hunting, as was her husband, though neither had done much, if any, turkey hunting. She asked most of the right questions about the tactics and strategies of calling in spring-season toms. The husband, having already seen two or three turkeys in the vicinity of camp on this first day, announced that tomorrow he would stalk one in the old-fashioned, sneak-up-on-them manner.

I don't know whether he had some ego hang-up about his lack of calling skills, or whether he considered turkey calling an affectation by those who sought to make hunting a turkey more difficult than it was, or whether he doubted, deep down, that calling really worked. I suspect it was all of the above.

Understand, I am not one of those who say, for safety or other reasons, that there is never a situation in which a hunter should try to stalk a gobbler. It depends on the time, the place, and the circumstances. It is not a wise idea in crowded public hunting areas, where it can result in injury or death to a hunter. This was not such an area. But in my mind, it also isn't the right way to go until sufficient efforts to call the bird have proven to be futile and the hunter decides that for his own personal purposes a dead turkey doesn't have to be one that comes to a call. An argument can even be made that in some ways it requires as much skill to silently sneak up within gun range of a wary tom turkey as it does to sit in one place and have the turkey come to you. But for most of us, it isn't the way the game is played.

After the husband went out the next morning and indeed succeeded in using ground contours and tree or brush cover to stalk and kill his gobbler, his conversation and demeanor indicated that he had concluded that his success proved his earlier presumption: Calling was overrated.

It bothered Doug, and to some extent, me. In a day and a half of hunting, neither of us had called in, much less pulled the trigger on, a gobbler.

As Doug sipped his peach brandy and I sipped my bourbon that night in the old mining shed, the lights from the two lanterns flickered off the corrugated metal walls, casting mournful-looking shadows. The mood was as dark and brooding as the shadows, and our lack of success so far, which wouldn't have troubled us otherwise, was grating on us because of the husband's attitude. Was some sort of paranoia setting in, or was it the 80 proof brandy and the 90 proof sour mash? Or all three? Doug was more quiet than usual, thinking perhaps of his father, and I blurted: "Let's go out in the morning and call in a couple of gobblers for the Colonel."

He looked up, at first glum, then brightening, and he said finally, "You know, that's a hell of an idea. Let's do it. Let's do it for Pap." (I thought of Dave Harbour as the Colonel; to Doug he was simply Pap.) Nothing more was said about it, but in effect a gauntlet had been laid down and there was a challenge to be met.

The predawn sky the next day was lightly overcast, but there was absolutely no wind and no rain. Just the invigorating chill of a spring morning in western turkey country. It would be a perfect morning for gobbling. Doug got into his truck, dropping the woman off at her station on the way, and went to his chosen spot. I got into my vehicle and went to my spot, driving down rut roads with only the parking lights on so as not to spook any roosted birds in the shadowy cottonwood trees in the distance. The trees were up where the east fork of the creek began to bend into the narrowing walls of the little side canyon. Up on the perpendicular cliffs just below the rim I knew that the figures of Indian hunters had been etched into the rock by long-ago Native civilizations. I wondered if some of the artists had been turkey hunters.

I parked the truck in some brush to hide it, dug out the fanny pack and the gun and the shells, loading one No. 4 into each chamber after I shut the back of the truck. I began walking down the trail, resisting the temptation to point a flashlight in front of me. The walk to within calling distance of the roost trees was made slightly more adventurous by the presence of a couple of belligerent Hereford bulls who finally got out of the way after staring straight at me and grunting with sullen menace for a minute.

I picked a small juniper to hide in, settled back, dug out a couple of rocks and sticks where my butt would have to rest for a while, laid the gun out beside me, and unzipped the fanny pack. I took out the Quaker Boy box call, a couple of diaphragms, and an owl hooter.

The eastern overcast was growing paler as I blew the classic notes of the barred owl into the hooter: "Who cooks for you? Who cooks for you-all?"

Two gobblers answered from my left, one about 150 yards away and the other, I guessed, about 100 yards farther up the creek. The closest one was so eager to respond that he almost cut off the end of the hoot; the other gobbled after the first one did.

When it was light enough to yelp without sounding like a hen that didn't have any better sense than to fly down in the darkness, I yelped. The nearer gobbler answered right back. This was starting to look like a piece of cake.

I don't know what happened to the far gobbler. But the near one flew down, went to the trouble to cross the creek, and headed straight for me. When he seemed almost to be in gun range, he stopped. The light was still very flat, and I could not be sure why the tom did it, but after gobbling once more he suddenly began circling to my right at exactly the perimeter at which he had initially stopped. And he did not look like he was going to do anything else but keep going.

There were some high weeds between me and him, but when he crossed into an opening, I pulled the trigger. I knew the range was marginal, but I had faith in the pattern of my 30-inch-barrel gun and its full-choke capability. It is a gun that had stood me in very good stead over the years on both geese and turkeys, some of which were killed at long ranges. I knew that it patterned more consistently at 30 to 45 yards than it did at 20 to 30. (There is a school of opinion that holds that short full-choke barrels, for instance 26 inches, are better for turkey hunting because they swing and point easier. My thinking is that we are not hunting doves or quail, where we must make quick snap shots at birds flying at unpredictable angles; we are in effect aiming the gun like a rifle most of the time, and therefore a long barrel provides a surer sighting plane.)

The turkey went down head over tail, feathers flying. I got up and ran toward him, because I realized that there was a good chance he wasn't hit hard enough at that range to make just one shot sufficient for a kill.

But a follow-up shot was unnecessary. I stood there over the bird, marveling once again at these supercharged moments in the hunting of what I consider to be the finest and most intriguing quarry that walks or flies. Thinking again of the Colonel, I knew that this kill would always be more special than others.

After I tagged the tom, unloaded the other shell, and gathered up the pack, I walked back to the little juniper where I had been sitting. I paced off the distance to the first blood spot I saw on the ground and the first loose feathers where the turkey initially went down. And in the gathering, brighter light, I could see now why he had hung up: There was a wall of low cactus down in the weeds between the juniper and the bird, and he either was dissuaded from crossing it or he had concluded that there was something very suspicious about a hen hiding in a juniper bush out there in a cactus-cluttered cow pasture.

And when I finally tiptoed over the cactus and counted off the paces, what I came up with was 63 yards.

Sixty-three yards. I sat down next to the turkey, hanging my head and shaking it, almost in shame. The earlier surge of excitement was giving way to something more sobering. If the Colonel was watching from somewhere, he surely was cringing. What in the name of ballistics had I been thinking about? The flat light and the fact that I have only one good eye (my depth perception has long since become an exercise in educated guesswork, even in the best of lighting conditions) had totally fooled me. I should never have shot in the first place, at least not until the turkey came closer, if he ever intended to. And I made a commitment at that moment never to make this mistake again. Somehow, I had gotten away with it. As it turned out, I discovered when cleaning the bird that a single No. 4 piece of lead had miraculously penetrated in just the right spot in the gobbler's head to ensure that there was no way he could have gotten away crippled. Had that lone piece of shot not struck him, it would have been a case of a complete miss.

When I pulled back into camp (it was about 8 A.M.), the feeling of having gotten blind-hog lucky without deserving it was replaced instantly by a new wave of jubilation. Because there, in his battered old pickup, was Doug, pulling into camp at the same time. I knew, particularly because of the vow we had made the night before, that there was no way he would quit this early without having tagged a gobbler.

Sure enough, his 18- to 20-pound tom, with a frayed 8-inch beard broomed off by brushing against a thousand rocks and his almost one-inch spurs, also dulled by rocky terrain, was virtually a twin of mine.

"Bob," he said, his voice alive with excitement, "I wish you could have seen it. This bird came in and walked up to within 25 yards of me and just stood there and strutted and gobbled. I thought of Pap and I decided to just let this gobbler do his thing as long as he would, just like Pap used to let them do. He liked to watch a gobbler, and he got to a point where it didn't matter if the tom got away or not.

"And so help me, it was just like that, just as if he was sitting there doing the calling for me. I bet I watched that bird for fifteen minutes before I finally took him."

We stood there over those gobblers and slapped hands, whooped, and laughed. We were both thinking about the Colonel, but neither of us made any further reference to him. We would talk quietly about it later, in the mining shed after supper, and maybe the schnapps and the bourbon would hold out.

Then the husband came out of the camping trailer, walked over, looked at the gobblers, and graciously congratulated us. I don't remember exactly what he said, but it was something like, "Obviously there's something to this calling business."

Good enough. After we hung our birds in the shady shed, I suggested to Doug that we drive up to where I had taken my gobbler. "You won't believe the range I shot at," I said, more sheepish now than I had been a few minutes earlier.

When we got to the area, I realized that there were more juniper bushes scattered around than I remembered. I couldn't quite pinpoint the one where I had sat. By now the sky was clearing, a breeze was blowing, and I guessed that most of the loose feathers had been scattered.

"Oh, there it is," Doug said, pointing. "You must have marked it."

There, in a high stand of weeds next to a short squatty juniper, was a foot-long tuft of toilet paper stuck like a flag to one of the tallest weed stalks. It looked as if somebody had tied it there about 3 feet off the ground.

It was my juniper, all right. I found the scuffed place where I had sat, the empty shell I had forgotten to pick up, the blood spots where the turkey had gone down, and what remained of the feathers. The little flag of white toilet paper fluttered in the breeze.

Doug looked at me quizzically. "Doug," I said, trying to keep my voice steady, "I didn't mark anything."

We looked at each other for several seconds, and I know that Doug was thinking of those tissue-paper markers that day a few weeks ago, hundreds of miles east in the Kansas turkey woods. It was as if the Colonel had left his signature on this hunt.

"You must have dropped it, or maybe you used it earlier and it blew into the weeds?" he said.

"I not only didn't use it," I said, "I didn't have any to use because I forgot to bring any with me." It was possible, of course, that this single piece of white tissue had blown from somewhere, although camp was at least a mile away, and just happened to hang up in a spot 6 feet from my juniper hiding place.

Make of this whatever you wish. Or make of it nothing at all. I understand. All I know is that we toasted the Colonel again that night, and the schnapps and bourbon gave out just about the time the Coleman lantern ran out of fuel.

7

IF A GOBBLER ANSWERS, DON'T HANG UP

BACK IN THE DARK AGES, in those ignorant years before I came to my senses and began to hunt turkeys, a friend who was organizing a turkey-calling contest got in touch with me.

"I'd like you to be a judge in the contest," he said, obviously making the fallacious assumption that the local outdoor writer was an expert on clucks, yelps, cackles, and gobbles.

"But I don't know how to call turkeys," I protested. "I don't even hunt them."

"No problem. You know what they sound like."

Actually, my auditory expertise with turkeys was confined mostly at that time to the barnyard variety. I probably had watched a TV show or two about turkey hunting, but I'm not even sure about that. Nonetheless, in a fit of generosity, I agreed to help my friend out.

And as I sat on one side of a curtain separating the judges from the callers, I had absolutely no trouble whatsoever: They all sounded like turkeys to me.

I say this in complete seriousness, with no disparagement whatsoever. I finally voted for somebody, but for all I know, he was the worst caller in the bunch.

The point is that you don't have to be an artist to appreciate art. You do not have to be a pianist to savor a piano concerto. You don't need to be a chicken to smell a rotten egg. Nor do you have to be an accomplished caller to go out and at least occasionally call in a turkey. Somewhere out there is a hot gobbler who, unlike me at the contest, isn't pretending to be an expert on turkey calling. He's just looking for company, and if the sounds you make at least suggest an invitation from the opposite sex, that's good enough for him.

Every top-notch turkey caller I ever talked to, including several professionals who design or manufacture calls and who compete in state and national contests every year, has said the same thing: In turkey hunting, calling is no more than 50 percent of the game. The rest is hunting savvy, position, strategy, and woodsmanship. But they are quick to add that calling is a very important 50 percent.

Absolutely. It is the element that brings the gobbler into gun range (unless you want to depend on guessing where he's going and then lie around waiting for him). It is the chief ingredient in the fascination of the sport, aside from the bird itself.

But dauntingly difficult and complex? No, it is not. Anyone who can move his hands in a coordinated manner or expell air over and past his tongue can call turkeys. If he sounds remotely like a gregarious hen, he has a chance to fool a gobbler.

There is a popular and frequently told anecdote (my guess is that it's apocryphal) that we may as well call "Gobblergate." I first heard this exploit attributed to the late Ben Rodgers Lee, who was one of the South's more famous turkey hunters, guides, and makers of calling devices.

Supposedly, Ben was hunting with another guy when they came to a closed fence gate that was between them and the spot they wanted to set up in. As Ben swung open the hinged gate, it creaked loudly. Instantly, a gobbler answered. Ben swung the gate again. The tom gobbled again, this time closer. Finally, as the two men lay on the ground, one pointing a shotgun and Ben swinging the rusty gate, they bagged the bird.

A dozen years after I first heard this yarn, a guy I know who has done a fair amount of turkey hunting, mostly in Texas, told me the exact same story, except that in this version he, not Ben Lee, was the protagonist. Ben Lee wasn't there.

If we gulp down the grains of salt, allow the benefit of the doubt, and assume that any of this ever happened, we also can assume that either the Gobblergate story is too delicious for some folks to resist indulging in blatant plagiarism, or that at least two gobblers in two separate places have been called in by squeaking rusty gates. (Is there a hinged-gate manufacturer out there somewhere who doesn't realize that he may have the patent on a turkey-calling gold mine?)

I, for one, am not so cynical or all-knowing as to discount the latter possibility, because some of the raspiest, screechingest, weirdest-sounding calls anybody ever created have been the downfall of a lot of gobblers. For that matter, some of the real hens in the woods sound worse than the worst caller I know.

Tom turkeys have been known to gobble back at slamming car doors, horns, sonic booms, whistles, thunderclaps, owls, crows, coyotes, mooing cows, and gunshots, to name just some of the sounds that are often referred to as "shock-gobble" noises. In other words, they shock the gobbler into gobbling.

But the main idea, and the one with consistent results, is to sound like a hen turkey. This isn't as difficult as it may at first seem to a beginning hunter. I know a guy who is now an experienced turkey hunter who went on his first spring hunt in northeastern Wyoming. At that time, his mouth-diaphragm yelps sounded something like a Holstein cow chomping loudly on a plastic cud. I know, because he demonstrated it for me. We are not talking here about anything with the classic *kee-oke, kee-oke* or *yawk, yawk* sound associated with yelping hens or imitations thereof. It was more like, "chuck, chuck, chuck," or "chomp, chomp, chomp."

But as he later told me, he was sitting up against a tree behind some brush on this Wyoming hillside, ruminating as loudly as he could. About midmorning he got sleepy. (Or maybe his jaws got tired.) Since he hadn't heard or seen a sign of a turkey and he had gotten very little sleep the night before, he figured a short nap wouldn't hurt anything. But he yelped (chomped) one more time before he let his heavy eyelids slap shut.

He had no more than nodded off before he was jolted awake by the sound of a gobbling turkey, one that was damned close. He made another couple of noises with his diaphragm and picked up his gun. Suddenly, a big gobbler appeared 50 yards in front of him, running, mind you, straight at him. He barely was able to get the gun up and yank the trigger in time to avoid becoming a statistic in the category of crimes known as turkey mugging.

Over the years he has become a much better caller, of course. We all do, if we stay with it.

I think where a lot of us go astray, at some point in our turkey-hunting lives, is when we try to closely imitate the expert callers we see and hear on TV shows, in videos, on tapes, or in calling contests. We aspire to be experts, too. These pros effortlessly create wonderful-sounding cackles, clucks, yelps, cutts, contentment purrs, whines, fighting purrs, gobbles, and a few sounds that I doubt a turkey ever made. Many of these callers seem to be particularly enamored of cackling with mouth diaphragms. That's a sound that hen turkeys occasionally do make, but not nearly so often as turkey callers do.

This is not to say that listening to tapes of turkeys and of callers imitating turkeys isn't a good place to start for a beginner. Short of getting hands-on instruction from an experienced friend, taped instruction is the best place to start. But don't get carried away with the more exotic renderings on some of these instructional tapes.

The truth, I'm convinced, is that the basic hen yelp will fool more gobblers than all the cutts and cackles and other calls put together. In second place I would rank the simple cluck, which is probably the most underutilized turkey call in the woods. It just ain't sexy-sounding enough. (To the hunter, that is.) You can't really lean into it like you can a cackle or a long series of yelps. Plus, a cluck that comes out wrong sounds like an alarm putt, and that's a sound to be avoided at all costs.

I'm also convinced that the most effective and reassuring (to the gobbler) type of calling device is the box caller, particularly those crafted out of cedar. It has its disadvantages, one being that it requires hand movement, which at the critical moment, when the gobbler is staring down your throat, can blow the whole shebang. Another disadvantage is that it can sort of spontaneously and accidentally emit a croak, screech, or putt from being shifted around in your pocket, or you can cause it to make such a noise just when you reach to extract it from a pocket. Again, an alarm putt is exactly what you don't want. Many hunters slip a muffling cloth or piece of tissue between the box paddle and the box itself to avoid committing this kind of faux pas.

But a good box has a realistic raspiness, and a child with a relaxed wrist can learn to use it sufficiently well to fool a turkey after thirty minutes of practice. Not every turkey, mind you, but a turkey somewhere, sometime.

I am reminded of the time my friend Doug roosted a gobbler and went to the spot before dawn the next morning. He had the bird pinpointed in a distant grove of cottonwoods. To get there, he had to ford a creek near the road. There were also cottonwoods at the ford, but so close to the road that they weren't often used as roost trees. Just to be sure, though, Doug owl-hooted before he walked up to the ford. And lo and behold, a gobbler answered back from a tree just on the other side of the ford.

Rather than plunge ahead and bump the bird off the roost, Doug decided to drop down behind the only cover within 50 yards, a single bush growing beside the two-track rut road leading to the ford. When it was light enough, he slipped a diaphragm yelper into his mouth and started calling.

The hot gobbler answered repeatedly and eventually flew down directly underneath the roost tree, which was on the other side of the creek. A lot of gobblers won't cross a creek to come to hen yelping. It's as if they are saying, "If one of us is going to get our feet wet or do any extracurricular flying, honey, it's going to be you, not me."

This tom strutted and fanned and gobbled in a grassy clearing under his roost tree while Doug gave him every variation of a mouth yelp and cackle that was in his repertoire. The bird simply was hung up, albeit only 70 yards away. Finally, in desperation, Doug reached for his old reliable Lynch Fool-Proof box caller. Only trouble was, he had lost the chalk for it and in its unchalked condition it sounded more like a screech than a yelp. He stroked the lid against the box anyway, four or five times in a row.

The tom went nuts, gobbling and strutting and looking decidedly more agitated. Doug gave him more of the same screechy yelps. The mouth diaphragm was forgotten. The tom trotted around to the rut road at the ford, waded across the shallow riffle, and came marching up the road on Doug's side of the creek. Doug dispatched him with a head-on shot at close range.

There is more than one lesson in this anecdote. One of them is that a box caller is hard to beat, with or without a fresh chalking job. Another is that when a gobbler has told you what song he wants to hear, give him plenty of the same music. Don't change the tune.

I think the next easiest and second most realistic sound comes from a slate caller. For some reason, there are gobblers who will absolutely commit themselves to the sounds of a deftly used slate but will do little more than gobble back infrequently and half-heartedly at a box. For purposes of creating a simple cluck or imitating the cutting of a boss hen or the purring of a contented hen, the slate is hard to beat. The disadvantages are, again, the necessity for hand movement and the fact that when some slates get wet or slightly greasy, they are worthless.

But if you want to be a complete turkey caller (this is not to say you aren't going to be successful anyway), you will want to learn to use a mouth yelper. A diaphragm. For one thing, it's so handy. You can carry one around in its plastic holder or simply slip it into your shirt pocket, then slip it out when you need to use it. Or, you can hold it lightly between your teeth as you go along, then slide it farther back into your mouth in calling position when you're set up and ready. When the turkey comes, if he does, you don't have to move your hands to send him a message.

Over the years I have become fairly proficient with a mouth yelper. There was about a three-week period after I first picked one up, however, when I didn't think this would ever come to pass. I spent most of those three weeks gagging. But one day a squawk emerged and things progressed from there.

I believe, though, that some turkeys in some areas of this country are becoming mouth-caller shy. They simply have heard too many of them, from too many diaphragm callers. It is not easy to duplicate the realistic raspiness of a box or a slate with a stretched piece of latex but, God knows, the mouth-yelper manufacturers are constantly trying, and some of them are doing a pretty fair job of it. There are single-reed diaphragms, double reeds, triple reeds, quadruple reeds, notched reeds, and, for all I know, reeds with a battery pack that do their own calling. But if you're calling turkeys with a mouth yelper and you aren't getting the responses you think you should, my advice is to fall back on a box or a slate.

The one characteristic of all hunters who are good at calling turkeys is their pace, or rhythm. When they are yelping, they may emit two yelps, or three, four, five, or even more, but what they all share is an instinctive sense of the crispness of the yelps and the timing between them. Listen to tapes of real turkeys and tapes of top-notch callers and you'll be surprised at the consistency.

Some hunters are so caught up in the calling mystique that they drive around town with yelpers in their mouths and practice at home until the wife, the kids, and the dog come at them with bared fangs. They buy every new caller that arrives on the market. Then they go out and fill the woods with yelps, cackles, and all manner of other avian noises, to the point of sounding like a barnyard full of hens that have lost their minds.

It is indeed possible to call too much. About the only time it isn't possible is on a very windy day. Since the sounds you are making in a stiff wind don't carry more than a third the distance they otherwise would, if that far, it pays to keep moving periodically and keep calling frequently until you hear a response. You may yelp during one gust and not be heard by a gobbler that's 200 yards away; twenty seconds later the wind may slack off and he can hear you fine. Try to time the yelps between the worst gusts.

For most hunters, the temptation to call too much comes when a gobbler is answering infrequently or intermittently. Even with a hung-up gobbler, one who seemingly refuses to come a step farther, incessant calling may be precisely the wrong thing to do. This simply further convinces the tom that his eager would-be companion is dying to join up with him and that if he just stands there and struts and gobbles once in a while she'll eventually find him.

The one type of caller that I never have been able to use effectively (let alone master) is the tube caller. I know that a tube can produce some awfully sweet, pure, clean notes that may be just the prescription for tickling the libido of a particular gobbler, but I just haven't succeeded so far in making my peace with tube devices.

Suffice to say that the bottom line on this calling business is to concentrate on what works for you, and what works for the gobbler.

In the immortal words of an editor I know, "Keep it simple, stupid."

8

CURSE OF OSCEOLA

WHEN JIM DONNELLAN PICKED UP BILL SHAPPELL and me at the Miami airport, there was a cooler of iced-down beer sitting in the backseat of his utility wagon. Having stood for ten minutes in the onslaught of tepid humidity that greeted us when we walked out of the terminal, his two guests from the polar regions of the Rocky Mountain West appreciated the gesture and promptly began popping a few tops on Mr. Busch's best.

We appreciated it even more as Jim, one of Miami's top lawyers and a man who is perfectly at ease in the hubbub that is Dade County, drove us deftly and aggressively through the conglomeration of traffic and humanity that clogs the Miami metropolitan area. At some point soon after we left the airport, the icy brew became more a tranquilizer than a coolant. Honking horns, screaming drivers, confusing signs, and complicated interchanges all blended into a witch's brew of racially diverse urbanism and freneticism not matched anywhere else this side of New York City. South Florida was just beginning to build its reputation as the land where tourists go to be mugged and have their cars hijacked. Instead of buying stone crabs, Cuban sandwiches, and bad Bloody Marys, some of them end up buying the farm.

It is also the land where avid turkey hunters go in search of the Osceola, or Florida turkey. This intriguing subspecies exists nowhere else but in Florida, although you can get an argument about the approximate latitude in midstate at which populations of the Eastern subspecies of the northern part of the state give way to the Osceolas of the central and southern parts. I suspect that a lot of would-be Grand Slam turkey hunters have gone home rejoicing over finally bagging an Osceola when what they really had was either a hybrid or an Eastern. Some hunters say there isn't much difference between the two subspecies, but experts know what the differences are and a layman generally concludes that Osceolas are smaller, longer-legged, darker, and more streamlined-looking.

There was no question what we would kill, if in fact we killed anything. Our hunt would take place on the northern reaches of the Big Cypress Swamp not far from the Big Cypress Seminole Indian Reservation, or about a half hour's drive south of Lake Okeechobee. The turkeys of the area are swamp turkeys and they are pureblood Osceolas.

Florida turkeys have a reputation among many hunters as the toughest-to-take turkeys in America. They are named for the great leader of the fierce Seminole uprising in Florida from about 1820 to 1838. Osceola held out for a long time. He was finally captured not by force but by deception: He was seized by U.S. military authorities while conferring under a flag of truce.

Force won't work, either, on the bird that is Osceola's namesake. And as the three of us were to learn on this hunt, they are getting pretty wise to deception, too. Flags of truce will be ignored. Bill, Jim, and I were to come to a complete understanding of the frustration Chief Osceola's pursuers must have felt.

We were hunting on a large ranch out of a trailer camp in a dense oak grove a short distance off a dirt road that was paralleled by a ditch. The ditch was home to alligators of various sizes, some of whom were even more impressive than the ones we had spotted in the bigger canals on the way up along Interstate Highway 75, otherwise known as Alligator Alley.

We stopped once at a truck stop beside the highway to gas up. A canal bordered the property and one of the biggest alligators any of us had ever seen was floating dead-still in the canal, eyes and the ridges of his backside protruding from the surface. He looked like he might be part of one of those "see the critter" roadside shows, except that in this case there was no pen or fence around him.

As Jim and I walked down to admire this paragon of reptilian repose, a woman tourist with what looked to be a four-year-old daughter in tow charged ahead of us down the path, and the child walked up to the edge of the water as if she were in a zoo. The gator glared balefully back at the girl, no more than 15 feet away.

Donnellan muttered under his breath and spoke loudly to the mother: "Ma'am, that alligator is dangerous. It's not a pet. Get the child away from the water."

The woman turned and looked at us with an expression of surprise. It was as if she only now realized that this was a real live alligator. She grabbed the girl by the hand and walked sheepishly back up the path to the gasoline pumps.

Jim briefed us a bit on Florida alligators and added this word of caution: "You need to watch for alligators while you're hunting in or around water."

Snakes?

"Not a problem. The feral hogs eat 'em and they've about got the snakes wiped out."

Feral hogs?

"Right," Jim said. "Some of them get to be three hundred pounds or more and you don't want to bump into one in a bad place. Particularly not a sow with her young."

Mosquitoes?

"They're always bad in the morning but it'll get better as the day goes on."

Alligators, wild boars, mosquitoes. Just a few of the inhabitants of this part of the world that make it interesting, along with the toughest turkeys in the land. But it is a beautiful, unique, and mysterious land, full of many forms of wildlife, and it impresses a first-time visitor so much that he, like Bill did, struggles to come up with the right word to describe it. "It's neat country," he said finally.

Indeed. It is a fascinating mixture of terrain, flora, and fauna, including grassy cattle pastures where various breeds of hamburger on the hoof graze around, closely followed by their ever-present companions the cattle egrets, snow-white birds that scuffle along beneath the bellies and legs of the cattle. Their purpose is to scarf up the grubs, worms, and bugs that the cattle kick over with their hooves.

The dry-land pastures are laced with canals and swamps and dotted with hammocks varying from backyard-size arbors to huge islands of trees, mostly moss-draped cypress but often including oaks, palms, and other varieties it would take a timber cruiser or a botanist to identify. Thick clumps of the ubiquitous palmettos usually fringe the hammocks, which may or may not be dry. The ones with the tallest, thickest cypresses are always dark inside, so dark even at high noon that regular camera film can't record an image without the assist of a flashbulb.

Many of the hammocks are torn up inside by the rootings of the feral hogs, and the loosened soil is black. Walking through a cypress hammock worked over by hogs is a little like negotiating a minefield that has been rototilled while wearing a blindfold. The mines, in this case, are the upright cypress knees (knobby growths springing from the roots) that are difficult to see in time to avoid adding yet another painful shin bark to your steadily growing collection of lower-leg bruises and scratches.

How did Chief Osceola curse us on this hunt? Let me count the ways. It got to be something of a prevailing camp joke. At one point Bill and I sat together behind a covering of palmetto fronds and watched a clearing. In the top of a dead snag about 30 yards away, three vultures perched.

"Do you think," I said to Bill, "they expect us to kill a turkey, or are they waiting for us to die?"

"I think," he said, "you got it right the second time."

Once, we decided to check out a power line right-of-way cut through swampy trees. We had gotten word that at least one big gobbler was using the area. Sure enough, there were large tracks etched in the mud of the rut road just before it disappeared for a ways beneath murky water about 6 inches deep. Jim suggested in a whisper that I go through or around the shallow swamp and head down the power line about 300 yards while he and Bill backtracked to another area.

I began hippety-hopping from clump to clump of cabbage weed, trying to keep the swamp water from going over my boot tops, when I saw a handy dark log to step on.

The log was unusually shiny and grayish black, like the water. It had funny-looking ridges on it.

It also had four legs, a long tail, and a jaw full of teeth. The log was an alligator.

One more stride and I would have stepped on the gator's head, unless he moved out of the way. And as I stood there balanced on one leg in my best imitation of an ostrich, he gave no indication of being inclined to do so. I understand that alligators often dispatch their larger prey by clamping onto some portion of the body, such as a leg, and then twisting and flopping in the water until the body part comes unscrewed.

I decided to damn the swamp water and go full speed in reverse. Finally, I found a way around the water and the alligator and reached a relatively dry area where I set up in three different spots and called for maybe a half hour in each place, to no avail. I later met my partners at an appointed rendezvous point. As we walked back to the vehicle we gave wide berth to a family of hogs consisting of a sow with her brood of piglets.

Spring turkey-hunting hours in Florida close at 1 P.M. That evening, we went through the usual camp skull session to decide where to hunt the next morning. I voted to forget the power line and go elsewhere, which was what we agreed to do.

We called in nothing the next morning, and when we got back to camp we bumped into a guide who was using the ranch. He had a hunter from another state in tow. The hunter had just bagged a beautiful gobbler with a 10-inch beard. Where, we asked, did the guy get the bird?

"Over there on that power line where the swamp crosses the road," he said.

I honestly can't say to what extent my close encounter with the alligator influenced my inclination to give up on the area, but it was a case of ignoring available evidence, the knowledge that a mature tom was in the vicinity, and going somewhere else based on no evidence at all. It was one of several mistakes and misfortunes that influenced the outcome of the hunt.

One morning we decided to return to an open dry area that was bounded on two sides by a thick forest and dotted in the middle by a cypress-hammock island. We had spooked two toms in the clearing earlier when we blundered through a ranch gate instead of first slipping through the palmettos to see if anything was out there.

A half hour before dawn the next day, I hunkered down in some tall, mosquito-infested grass at the edge of a cattle-watering tank that was about 50 yards east of the hammock. The mosquitoes whined around my ears and found ways to drill through the camouflage mask I wore under my camo cap.

Getting to this position, I had just had one of the weirder experiences of all my turkey-hunting years. As I walked in the predawn darkness across the grassy flat leading to the water tank, my ears were assaulted by the barking and howling of what obviously were a couple of wild dogs.

They bayed like hounds on the trail of a fox, a rabbit, or a raccoon. The noise was getting louder, and the chase (I later concluded it must have been the pursuit of a white-tailed deer) seemed headed directly at me. I never saw the deer, but just after I slipped two magnum No. 4s into my over-under (if I am going to be mugged by wild dogs, I am sure as hell going to let them know I am armed and somewhat dangerous), I saw the dogs, running full-out and howling like the hounds of hell, suddenly veer to my left and gradually progress almost out of earshot.

It was therefore with some surpise that when I sat down in the weeds, waited a half hour, and then used my mouth yelper to give a couple of fairly soft tree calls, I heard a gobbler answer immediately from one of the tall cypress trees at the far end of the hammock.

There is no doubt that the tom had heard the canine cacophony. But sitting safely in his roost, he obviously had concluded that the danger was past. Now his mind was back on prospects for the morning's social activities.

I sat there for maybe thirty more minutes—while the mosquitoes stormed the camo-clothing moat and breached the walls of the repellent-fortified castle, and played out one of those "Here I am" and "Yes, and HERE I am," exchanges with the tom. It was time to make a decision: Hold my ground and wait to see if the gobbler finally would come the 300 yards to my position or lose interest and go somewhere else; or meet him about halfway before he could decide to go somewhere else.

I chose the latter course. Stooped over like Quasimodo prowling the bell tower of Notre Dame, I creeped to the edge of the dark hammock and entered it. It was almost full daylight, but the blackness inside the hammock was disconcerting. Trying gingerly to avoid the cypress knees, I paused in the middle of the hammock and yelped, and got an answer.

Picking a spot on the perimeter of the cypress trees about halfway between my original position and the gobbler, I sat down in front of a tree trunk and cut half a dozen palmetto stalks to plant in front of me, whittling the base of each stalk down into a sharp point so as to drive it into the ground.

Then I yelped again. And got absolutely nothing back in return.

There were three main possibilities: The tom was on his way, he had been spooked, or he had joined up with one or more hens. Maybe he had simply decided that there was something suspicious about this whole scenario and that the prudent course of action might be to stroll away and seek other companionship.

After twenty minutes it was apparent he wasn't coming. I walked slowly back into the dim interior of the hammock and plodded toward the east end of it, hoping that if I set up at that end and called, I might get a response from somewhere.

When I got to the end I was greeted with the approach of the truck occupied by my two partners. They had circled the hammock in the truck looking for me, having decided that the earlier noisy intrusion of the wild dogs must have totally spooked every turkey in hearing distance into fleeing for other environs.

We can rehash and anguish over these little tragedies all we want, but most of the time we can never be sure exactly what went wrong. The gobbler I was working may have been spooked by the sight or sound of the truck, or he may simply have lost interest and departed.

If the latter was the case, it could have had something to do with my choice of calling device, a mouth diaphragm. I was told later by an experienced south Florida guide that Osceola turkeys tend to be shy of mouth callers in general and too much calling in particular. I certainly had done a fair amount of mouth calling in trying to work this tom. As the guide explained, his experience, and the experience of many hunters he knows who chase Osceolas, is that these turkeys don't gobble much, and when they do gobble, they do it mostly from the roost. If they gobble from the ground, it is in answer to the first call from a box caller, not from a diaphragm. And they often gobble only once. Then, if they come, they come silently. A wise south Florida hunter, the guide said, strokes his box caller softly and not very often, and then he sits back, watches, and waits.

I believe him. I certainly have no refuting data to offer, nor am I able to this day to produce the tail fan or beard of an Osceola gobbler. I still can't give you a conclusive opinion on whether Osceola turkeys are the toughest turkeys to hunt in the United States, but they are plenty tough enough and they certainly have some advantages: They don't gobble much and they move about like ghosts. Because of the natural cover and the swampy obstacles, they are neither easy to spot nor easy to get to if you hear one. There is so damned much out there for them to hide in.

But there was something at work on this totally unsuccessful hunt that went beyond the hunting conditions, the habits and tendencies of the bird, and the ignorance and poor strategy on the part of the hunters. It seemed to even go beyond bad luck.

One day we drove back to camp about a half hour before the 1 P.M. daily closure, having been drenched by a half-hour downpour that must have dumped an inch of rain. Florida is supposed to be the Sunshine State, but don't be taken in by the chamber of commerce scam. My experience in South Florida is that it rains there for some period of time, maybe five minutes, maybe five hours, maybe something in between, virtually every day. And nowhere in God's turkey country does it rain harder than it does in South Florida.

Anyway, on the way back we stopped about a half mile short of camp to check out a couple of ponds where we figured we might catch some largemouth bass that evening. As Jim parked the truck, I asked, "Should I bring my gun?"

"Nah," Jim said. "No use."

When we walked up to the first pond, a gobbler stepped out of the brush fringing the pond and stood there, staring at us. He was at marginal shotgun range and it may have been that he was too far away even for magnum 4s, but he was *definitely* too far away to be nailed with a thrown pocketknife, which was the only weapon I had in my possession.

"Nah," Jim muttered, shaking his head, "whatever you do, don't bring your gun."

Somewhere, a great chief named Osceola was smiling.

9

A DOUBLE WHAMMY

AFTER ALL THESE YEARS, I'm still not totally sure what I think of hunting turkeys in pairs (the hunters are in pairs, not the turkeys). But I am getting close to concluding that except for instructional purposes, certain tactical situations, or pressing considerations, it ought to be avoided.

First off, there's the question of what I mean by hunting in pairs, or to put it another way, double-team hunting. Just to clarify it, it doesn't mean going to the hunting area camping and/or scouting with a partner. It doesn't mean sharing camp chores and food and drink and being there to listen to the other's tales of woe, excuses, or narratives of triumph. Hunting in pairs also doesn't mean sitting around with a couple of bourbons or cups of coffee in hand, cooperatively plotting and think-tanking the next morning's hunt.

All of these are pleasant by-products of the hunt, of course. There are bonuses to having somebody accompany you on a hunt. You can slap your own hands after you kill a gobbler, but it just isn't the same as slapping somebody else's, particularly if that somebody understands all the trouble you went to in order to bag this bird.

Double-team hunting means that you and your partner go out and stick together like a couple of licked postage stamps placed back to back, one or both of you doing the calling and one or both of you ready to do the shooting.

Some very exciting and satisfying moments in gobbler hunting have come to me while hunting with a partner, particularly on those occasions when I was simply doing the calling and trying to help him get his turkey. Those sorts of moments often come when double-team turkey hunting involves an experienced hunter-caller introducing a newcomer to the sport.

I have absolutely no problem with this scenario. Somebody had to show me how it was done, introduce me to the mechanics and the mysticism, and I am eternally grateful that somebody did. The least I can do, if a beginner asks me, is to be as generous as my initial benefactor was. It's a sort of repayment of a debt.

If everything goes well on a double-team hunt, there is a shared memory that becomes all the more joyful to recount because it happened to both of you at the same time, in the same place. But if something goes wrong, there is a tendency (however muted) to indulge in second-guessing and recriminations, to wonder whether, if you had been out there by yourself, things would have turned out differently.

The first problem with double-teaming is that it increases the chances of being heard or seen by a factor that is probably much larger than two. Because the hunters are moving around together, talking and whispering and gesturing, they may be five times as likely to be detected by a gobbler or his hens.

The second big problem is that instead of simply clarifying in your own mind what *you* are going to do when presented with the chance to call a gobbler (or as they say in basketball, when you get to "crunch time"), you and your partner have to come to a meeting of the minds. This, at the very least, requires gestures and whispers, unless both of you are lip-readers who don't need voices to communicate.

Who is going to do the calling? Who is going to do the shooting? Both? Or one or the other? Is it first-volley, first-served? Or does one guy only shoot as a backup? Or does he not shoot at all? Do you decide this at the last minute? ("You take him, he's on your side.") Or do you decide it well in advance?

Actually, the most important thing is that you decide it—at whatever point. Don't try to guess or assume what the other guy is thinking or understanding. I have to concede that last-second whisperings, when a gobbler crosses the magic yard line that separates wishful thinking from effective range, don't often spook the turkey. I am not at all sure that turkeys understand the meaning of the human voice when it is delivered in a stage whisper. I have whispered to the guy on my right, or my left, when the gobbler or gobblers were within 35 yards or less, and as near as I could tell, there was no reaction from the turkeys.

But what does spook turkeys is movement, or shapes or colors that seem to be out of place. If one hunter squirms or shifts at the wrong moment, or brings his gun up when the gobbler is looking, somebody is going to be shooting at a running or flying turkey, if there's a chance to get off a shot at all.

If one hunter moves or makes a mistake such as forgetting to slip on his face mask or otherwise screws up the works, there are bound to be some awkward moments, and regretful thoughts, later. Or, if one hunter acts as a backup and ends up firing the shot that actually hits and kills the turkey, it helps if the two of you are very close friends. If everything isn't agreed upon in advance, it is possible in some situations for one of the hunters to fire a shot a second or a split second before the other one was about to pull his trigger (on either his first or on a follow-up shot), and then there is the question of whether the successful shooter was trying to shortstop the other one. The issue tends to lie there conspicuously, like a dog turd on somebody's living room carpet.

There are a couple of advantages to double-team hunting, however. One is that four eyes and four ears are more likely to see or hear something than two eyes and two ears. The biggest and most beautiful Rio Grande gobbler I ever saw was killed by a friend of mine who has excellent eyesight—far better than mine. I was doing the calling for him in a grove of cottonwood trees with an understory of fairly thick brush. At one point I thought I heard a turkey cluck (it was windy and I couldn't be sure), but I never saw anything or even became aware there was a turkey in gun range until my partner whispered that he was about to shoot. He was the designated shooter anyway, which was damned lucky, because I never saw the gobbler at all until I walked up to where it was flopping behind a bush that had partly obscured my view.

Another advantage is one that doesn't happen very often, but when it does it significantly decreases the gobbler's chances of escape: One hunter shoots right-handed and the other shoots left-handed.

Every turkey hunter who has spent much time at the sport has experienced a gobbler walking up on the shooter's off side. In other words, if the shooter is right-handed (and can swing the gun to his left easily but not very far to his right), the gobbler approaches from the extreme right. When that happens, you have three options: One, you can wait and hope the gobbler wanders around into the center portion or left side of your comfortable field of fire; two, you can squirm or wheel around if the gobbler's line of sight is temporarily obstructed; or three, if you have had some practice at it, you can very slowly inch the gun butt over to your other shoulder and shoot him left-handed. (I don't place much faith in the average shooter's ability to accomplish number three.)

But if two guys are hunting together and one happens to be right-handed and the other is left-handed, the two of you can position yourselves so that one shooter covers the area from the center to the extreme left, and the other covers the center over to the extreme right. The only way one of you can't shoot easily is if the gobbler walks up behind both of you.

But misunderstandings and miscalculations can occur even when the double team is ambidextrous, so to speak. It happened to a partner and me when, as we were nearing a gobbling turkey, I made the mistake of suggesting my partner sit down against a tree slightly ahead of me and about 10 yards to the right of the tree I sat down against. The only problem was that, as I soon realized, I am a left-handed shooter and he is a right-handed shooter. I should have sat down where he sat down, and vice versa.

There was a wall of high, thick weeds straight in front of us, and the gobbler was already on his way in answer to my box-caller yelps. In a moment or two he would be in range. But I knew he wasn't likely to plow through the weeds: He would go around to our left or to our right. If he went to the extreme right, most likely I would have to shoot him, even though I was 10 yards farther away, because my partner probably wouldn't be able to get around in position for a shot without the risk of spooking the bird.

We had flipped a coin earlier, shortly after we first heard the tom gobble, and my partner had won. He was supposed to shoot first. But as we sat there waiting, I whispered, "If he comes around way to the right, I'll shoot."

I remember him whispering his okay to this. So when the turkey came around way to the right and at a bit of an angle behind us and got into an opening where I could shoot him, I shot. The trouble was, I didn't kill him, but my partner, who had alertly kept his gun at the ready when we stood up, was able to kill him with a fine shot at a bird running away as fast as a turkey can run.

"I was just about to shoot when you shot," he said.

I had made a second mistake, aside from sitting in the wrong place, of having assumed that my partner wouldn't be able to shift around. I had stopped looking at him and was concentrating on watching the oncoming gobbler. Therefore, I missed the fact that when the turkey was behind some cover, my partner had been able to squirm all the way around and get in position to shoot to his extreme right.

Even though the turkey was in the bag and there was no question who killed it, the way it happened created an uncomfortable moment and a fair amount of second-guessing, mostly of the self-inflicted variety. And although our friendship is too old and too strong to be jeopardized by what happens with a turkey, I would just as soon the incident had never happened at all. What I really wish is that I had looked over and seen that the other hunter was in position to shoot. Then I wouldn't have shot at all.

The fact is that hunting and calling turkeys is totally unlike sex, ballroom dancing, arm wrestling, dove hunting, marriage, tennis, badminton, volleyball, and a long list of other activities in this respect: It is most rewarding when done alone. It becomes a very personal and introspective experience that is all the more rewarding for the fact that it happened to you and you alone, and the success or failure of it was caused by you and you alone.

At some point, the person who is struggling to make the transition from bumbling clueless beginner to experienced turkey hunter has to go out on his or her own. He must leave the double-team concept behind and progress onward to solitary satisfaction.

You can depend forever, I guess—if you have some very patient friends who are accomplished turkey hunters—on somebody else to do the calling for you, to analyze the situation for you, to pick the hunting spot for you, to roost the birds for you, and to get you in position to pull the trigger.

If you do this, you may be a turkey killer, but you aren't really a turkey hunter. You are a dilettante, a parvenu, messing around with something you really don't understand or love.

There are times, of course, if you make the progression to skilled turkey hunter, when you will do, achieve, or experience something that makes you wish somebody had been there to witness it. Hunters of other species, or anglers, experience the same feeling when they know they have done their absolute best and have been rewarded for it. But then they take a second reading and realize that, had they not been alone, maybe they wouldn't have been as keen and sharp and innovative.

In the long run, the only person in this world you can absolutely be sure of fulfilling or impressing is yourself. And you can do that, with or without witnesses. In some respects it is even more rewarding when you do a fine thing alone, because there is nobody around to judge it on its merits but yourself and nobody you have to thank for helping you do it. There is no need to embellish it because it is perfectly satisfying the way it is.

When I am hunting alone I have this strange, brief, aboriginal (some might say so, anyway) ritual I usually go through when I kill a turkey, particularly if it is one I have had to work a little harder for than another: I walk or run up to the downed turkey, and when I am satisfied that the shot has resulted in a swift, merciful kill, I put down the gun and yell. Just yell, once and briefly. I guess the word that comes out, is "YEAH!" It is like a primitive "All right, you did it" message delivered to the world in general—whether the world hears it or not, or cares or not. This might be perceived by somebody else as a sign of disrespect for the bird, but actually it is the opposite. If I had no respect, if there were no challenge involved, if there were no chance the bird would beat me in this confrontation that I have initiated, I would have no exhilaration.

The exhilaration is always followed by a quiet period of reflection and admiration for the quarry. I know that there will continue to be those times when the bird whips me, fairly and squarely, and if gobblers could yell, I would have no problem at all with being yelled back at as the bird disappears in the distance. Sometimes I think they do yell: You get that last sort of dismissive gobble that tells you this turkey has your number.

But when I beat the turkey and I do it alone, the whole affair is far more satisfying, in a very personal way, than if I had done it in the presence of a stadium packed with eighty thousand witnesses.

10

SAFETY FIRST

I ONCE READ A STORY in an outdoor magazine written by a turkey hunter who said he sat in one spot in Pennsylvania and called in nine consecutive two-legged creatures that responded to his hen yelps. But they weren't gobblers, they were hunters.

This all happened in a single morning. This story raises all sorts of questions having to do with safety, one of which is the first that occurred to me: Why the hell would he sit there and call long enough to lure in nine hunters? I would have been out of there, at the latest, after the second one. Being the object of the desires of a small army of individuals toting shotguns is too much like being a turkey to suit me, and I don't have near the woods-wisdom or escapability of a turkey. I would have been just a tad nervous about my well-being long before the second guy showed up.

Then again, maybe the author of this story was potentially sacrificing himself in the name of research in order to help with answers to some of the other questions: One, how dangerous is this sport we call turkey hunting? Two, has it become more or less dangerous with the tremendous growth in turkey-hunting participation in the past twenty years? Three, to the extent it is dangerous, why is it that way? And finally, four, what can we as turkey hunters do about it? There also are all sorts of ancillary questions here, such as why would any gobbler hunter stalk the sound of hen yelps?

I have heard lots of answers to and comments on some of these very serious questions. Some of the answers make a lot of sense. Some don't. Among the ones that don't are suggestions that we all ought to be out there wearing fluorescent orange, otherwise known as hunter-safety orange or blaze orange. Some of the thinking along these lines is that if you wear camouflage-pattern blaze orange you're probably just as camouflaged as if you were wearing hunter brown or hunter green or tree-bark camo, because turkeys are color blind, or at least see colors in shades of gray.

I don't believe that theory for a minute, although I have no way to disprove it. There are eye physicians and avian biologists who can expound on the exact physical makeup and capabilities of the wild turkey's eye, but anybody who wanders around in turkey woods wearing blaze orange is like a golfer carrying nothing but a putter as far as I'm concerned. He is seriously handicapping himself. The game is tough enough already.

There are times when fluorescent orange can help insure your safety on a turkey hunt, times when you aren't in the actual act of hunting (more on that in a bit). But if colors don't mean anything to turkeys, why is it that (particularly in the spring) the male of the species is so much more colorful than the hen, with iridescent feathers and flaming red, bright blue, and glaring white in his head and neck? You don't suppose it's because the turkeys, hens or toms, can tell the difference, even from a distance, do you? For that matter, if birds are color blind, why is it that in many bird species the male is so much more brilliantly colored than the female? Surely this isn't just to impress the binocular-equipped bird-watchers among us. Why is it that hummingbirds go to red feeders and red flowers?

Nonetheless, the fact is that spring turkey hunting, wherein effective ranges are primarily within 40 yards and the tactical idea is to hide and sound like a turkey, is more dangerous than most other forms of hunting. The percentage of hunters injured or killed while turkey huntiong is higher than in, for example, deer hunting or duck hunting. Deer, in fact, appear to be color blind, which would help explain why so many orange-clad hunters kill so many deer.

In how many other types of hunting, besides turkey hunting, does the hunter in effect disguise or represent himself as the hunted? Not many, although duck, deer, and elk hunters, for example, often try to call in their quarry with sounds mimicking those species. Hunters bugling like a bull elk have been killed by other hunters, and so, alas, have turkey hunters attempting to sound like either hen turkeys or gobblers. On the other hand, squirrel hunters may try to chatter like squirrels and duck hunters may try to sound like lonesome ducks, but they are not likely to be shot by somebody mistaking them for squirrels or ducks.

I do believe that measures to make turkey hunting as safe as possible have grown significantly as the sport—which now attracts more than two million participants—has continued to grow. Many states have outlawed the use of rifles and many have set restrictions on legal shotgun loads, disallowing buckshot and certain other large shot sizes. The temptation to take a 60-yard or longer potshot at a turkey diminishes accordingly, and your chances of surviving a direct hit from, say, a load of No. 4s or 6s are presumably higher than if the load carried No. 4 buckshot or BBs.

All sorts of supposedly etched-in-granite rules have been proffered as the commandments that will prevent turkey-hunting tragedies. Some of these rules are at best flexible, if not downright questionable. But one that can't be questioned is, *make sure of what you are shooting.* Assuming hen turkeys aren't legal game (in the spring it's gobblers only, although hens may be legal in the fall season), *identify it as a gobbler. See the gobbler's beard.*

See the beard. Those three words will save you the chagrin, embarrassment, guilt, and (in most instances) illegality of shooting a hen by mistake. Mistakes can be made, of course, even by experienced hunters, but if there is any doubt at all about the sex of the turkey you are about to shoot, don't.

Far more critical than the mistake of shooting the wrong bird is the horrible misjudgment that could cost somebody his or her life or inflict hideous injury. *See the beard* is still a good rule of thumb for avoiding such a catastrophe, but it's not the only rule and by itself can't guarantee a safe hunt. Nevertheless, the point is that any hunter taking enough pains to make sure of the sex of the bird he sees, or thinks he sees, is taking enough pains to make sure it's a turkey in the first place. He is not shooting at shapes or movement or sounds.

That's one of the reasons I have a strong dislike for the practice commonly known as "party hunting," as it applies mainly to deer and elk hunting. This misbegotten tradition involves a group of hunters in which one or more have licenses for a buck or bull and one or more others have licenses allowing the taking of a doe deer or cow elk. The idea in their minds is to shoot whatever happens along, then sort out the proper tags and sexes later. In addition to being unethical, illegal, and wasteful (if there are more carcasses than tags to match), it's dangerous.

The danger factor here is that somebody who doesn't care what sex of animal he is about to shoot may not be looking closely enough to tell if it's a deer or elk in the first place, instead of a man or something else.

Do not believe that a very dangerous situation can't crop up in your turkey hunt. Let me relate a personal experience:

One spring I was the guest of a group of hunters in northern Missouri. The hunt was on private land and the host was one of the owners of a turkey-hunting-equipment company. It was not until I and my traveling partner (who had hunted this property once before) arrived that we learned that, counting the two of us, there were some dozen hunters who would be hunting at the same time on no more than 1,500 acres of heavily timbered land. Although some of us would be hunting in pairs (thus cutting some territorial slack), this technically figures out to not much more than 100 acres per hunter, a narrow margin for error or confusion. Realizing this, the host each night assigned each hunter or two-hunter team to a specific spot on the property and asked that we not stray much from those spots. This would not be a hunt in which any hunter hearing a gobble a half mile away could go directly to the gobbler without fear of bumping into or interfering with another hunter.

Our generous host issued all his guests a box caller, camo pants and shirt, a fluorescent orange carrying bag or knapsack in which to carry any turkey that might be killed, and a small white decal about the size of a dime. In black letters on the decal were the words "Be Safe." The decal was to be placed on the upper front part of the stock, or the tang, of the hunter's shotgun.

The first morning, my partner and I went to our assigned area. We decided to hunt and call together, since I knew nothing about the lay of the land.

We heard a turkey gobble in a dense stand of trees a short distance across a shallow hollow. We sat down and began to call, and the gobbler answered back immediately. His next gobbles sounded closer. This was beginning to look like a tailor-made setup, and we hadn't strayed out of our assigned zone.

Then there was complete silence. Both of us understood that this wasn't necessarily a bad sign. A gobbler that has pinpointed the location of a hen yelp sometimes shuts up and comes the rest of the way strutting and fanning, but not gobbling again. Peering intently into the dense maze of tree trunks across the hollow, my companion (we had agreed that he would call and I would shoot) said, "I see him."

I looked where he was looking, and saw dark movement in the trees maybe 60 yards away. Something was walking at an angle through the trees, not exactly straight down the slope toward us, but in our general direction, and there was no doubt in either of our minds that it was the oncoming gobbler. A moment later, I saw what appeared to be the black-bronze feathering of a turkey, and the shape seemed to be bobbing a bit, as a turkey does when it walks and is craning its neck to find another turkey. There was a maze of slender tree trunks out in front of us and it was difficult to make out a distinct shape.

"Wait and be sure," my partner said, and I knew that he was referring primarily to making sure that it was, one, a gobbler, not a hen, and two, a mature gobbler and not a jake, which I didn't particularly want to shoot on the first morning of the hunt. I was looking right down the barrel at the oncoming shape and all I was waiting to do was make certain that this indeed was a mature tom and that he was in effective range. I still hadn't made out the whole distinct shape of a gobbler or seen his beard.

My companion let out a gasp and then said, in a clear, loud voice, "My God, it's a man."

Indeed it was. One of the other hunters on the property was walking down a trail in our direction, carrying a dead Eastern-strain gobbler over his shoulder. The dangling head of the turkey bobbed, and as the hunter got closer I could even see the beard protruding from the turkey. The fact that the hunter was camo-clad had made his form blend into the green background, whereas the turkey's colors stood out.

I was stunned into silence, sitting there thinking that although I was not on the verge of pulling the trigger, I was not that very

far away from it, either. I wouldn't have pulled it even if my partner had said nothing because I had figured out what was happening in the same instant that he did, and I have never yet fired at an
upside down gobbler. But I had aimed a shotgun at a human being
for several seconds, and I couldn't help wondering what an inex-
perienced hunter might have done.

I looked down at the top of the forestock of my over-under,
and the little white decal flashed back at me: *Be Safe.*

When I stood up, my knees were weak. We called out to the
guy carrying the turkey, walked over to him, and told him what
had happened.

What had happened, aside from him walking toward a pointed
shotgun, was that he had killed his gobbler about a half hour previously and was taking a shortcut back to camp headquarters with
it. There was no doubt that we had heard a gobbler answering our
yelps. The guy with the turkey said he had heard the gobbler himself. Yet it had not occurred to him that he might be walking
straight into another hunter. The gobbler no doubt had spooked at
his approach, which was why the bird had shut up abruptly.

Although all the hunters in camp had clear-cut understandings
on where to hunt, we had not covered the contingency of where
to walk, or when to do it, in the event of having to hike across
country back to camp after bagging a gobbler.

Compounding all of this was the fact that the successful hunter,
who looked shaken when we told him we thought he was an
oncoming gobbler, had failed to pack along his fluorescent orange
knapsack, specifically designed to help the hunter safely carry a bird
out of the woods. This man had absentmindedly left his at camp
headquarters.

He would have been totally safe if he had remembered the
knapsack and stuffed the bird in it. He would have been almost as
safe if he had simply packed along a fluorescent orange cap and
worn it in place of his camo cap as he carried the bird, or tied an
orange cloth or ribbon to the bird. Of course, there are hunting

areas where, because of low hunting pressure, these measures probably aren't necessary and walking out in the open with a gobbler
over one's shoulder is a lot safer than walking through trees and
brush with it.

I still shudder when I think of that incident in Missouri. I have
had the distasteful, sad task of reporting stories on fatal or near-fatal
turkey-hunting accidents, and the incident I had been involved in
was a hell of a lot more conducive to producing disaster than some
of the ones I knew about that *had* produced disaster.

I know of a hunter who shot and seriously wounded his
brother, who was crawling toward him while making gobbling
sounds. As near as I could tell after reading the facts of the case,
both hunters were at fault to some degree, but the wounded man
ended up suing his own brother.

In another tragic incident, two hunters who were sitting down
making hen-yelp calls during a fall season were shot in the head by
an elderly hunter who fired at them with buckshot after he swore
he saw two turkeys in the brush. One hunter was killed and the
other severely wounded. At that time, the state in which this took
place allowed buckshot for turkey hunting. Now, nothing larger
than No. 2 shot is legal there. The injured man eventually got out
of the hospital but never fully recovered from the effects of the
blast.

Some of the rules commonly listed as safeguards against possible tragedies are these:

1. Never stalk a turkey.
2. Don't make gobbling sounds.
3. Never wear red, white, or blue, the colors of a turkey's head
   and neck.
4. Always make sure of your target (again, *see the beard*).
5. When another hunter approaches your calling or hiding
   spot, don't stand up suddenly or make any other movement
   until you have called out in a loud voice that you are there
   and have gotten an acknowledgment.

6. Never play a "joke" on a partner by making calls that he can hear.
7. Try to select a calling spot with something protecting your back, such as a tree trunk.

These are all useful axioms, and some are imperative in avoiding hazardous situations, but the first two are a little too arbitrary, in my opinion. Never stalk a turkey? What's the definition of "stalk?" Getting closer? There are situations, even in calling to a gobbler, in which the hunter, if he is going to be successful, has to sneak toward the bird to get into another position, or perhaps even to get close enough to shoot, if the tom has hung up just slightly out of sure gun range. And in this context I'm talking a matter of a few yards, not hundreds of yards.

Many of us have come to look disdainfully upon stalking as an unethical way of hunting (turkeys, that is), but if stalking as such were unethical, most of the big-game hunters in America would be unethical. The use of stalking tactics must be placed in the context of the situation and the possible compromises of safety, but if stalking by itself is unsafe, so is simply walking quietly through the woods. The question is, What are you stalking and why? Are you sure of what you are stalking, or are you just sneaking in the direction of a sound you heard? In no instance should you be stalking the sound of a hen. And if you're a true spring turkey hunter, you are there to call in a bird and have the enjoyment of seeing it come in, not to slip up on it and shoot it.

But moving in the direction of a gobble? Absolutely, if you think you're too far away to call when you first hear it, or the spot you're in isn't a good hiding place that leaves the gobbler a fairly unobstructed path to you when you do start to call.

Making gobbling sounds with a box, a shaker, or other device? Yes, if the situation calls for it and all other tactics have failed. But outside of using the gobble as a locater call before dawn or after dusk, the times when it's called for are relatively rare, and there better be some careful consideration given to your location and surroundings. Are you hunting on lightly pressured private land, or heavily hunted public land? Are there other hunters nearby, and if so, are they trusted members of your own party who are not going to try to stalk within shooting range of a gobbling tom, or are they strangers who might just crawl up with a gun in their hands? If you are any good at all at imitating a gobble, another hunter is just as likely to take you for a turkey as a turkey is—probably more so.

When to use a gobble? Again, my feeling is that it's most useful in trying to pinpoint the locations of roosted gobblers, usually right at dark or shortly after dark. Gobblers that have just gone to roost sometimes like to assert their territories to rival toms. The gobble isn't usually necessary as a locater call in the morning, because most gobblers will respond to an owl hoot or a crow call during this period.

There is another situation in which a gobble call may be useful, and that's when a hunter is having no success enticing a harem-boss tom away from his hens. Most hunters have heard of the tactic of gobbling to stir up the boss tom's jealous aggressiveness, and it may on rare occasions actually work, bringing him charging in your direction.

But again, it pays to be judicious in the times and places you use a gobble for this purpose, and my experience tells me that it isn't nearly as likely to produce results as is the patience it takes to keep calling to the assembled hens with various sorts of hen talk. Get them interested, or jealous, or mad, or curious, and they may amble over to see what all the fuss is about. If they do, the gobbler is almost sure to come with them.

You are seldom certain whether the gobbler you are seeing is the dominant gobbler in the harem, anyway. If there's another one around (and he may or may not be visible to you), he could be the harem boss and the designated butt kicker of the neighborhood, which means that gobbling at the subordinate tom is more likely to send the subordinate retreating in the opposite direction than to bring him to you.

If there's a bottom line, the best I can come up with is this thought: There isn't a gobbler in the world, or ten gobblers, or any number of gobblers, that are worth taking one gamble, cutting one corner, making one miscalculated assumption or one hasty decision that could result in someone's injury or death.

11

GUIDING LIGHT

I HAVE ALWAYS RESPECTED and admired the professional men and women who make their livings guiding hunters and anglers to the game or the fish. There are a few bad apples in the profession (as there are in any other form of economic endeavor), but the true professional guides are people who are knowledgeable, skilled, and responsible. In some instances they don't get paid what they are really worth.

From time to time I get calls from persons who ask about the fees charged for guided fishing or hunting trips. When I tell them what the going rates are, the response they give me often goes something like this: "Wow. That's pretty steep. I just want to have some fun in the outdoors. This is a vacation to me." There is the unspoken inference that because the paid-for service involves hunting and fishing, instead of something like brain surgery or legal representation, it ain't really all that serious and therefore shouldn't involve serious money.

But it's not a vacation to your guide or your outfitter. It's his or her profession and livelihood. Not only that, but he or she assumes a heavy responsibility not only for your recreational pleasure but in many respects for your safety. Liability insurance, bonds, and licenses are part of a guide's or outfitter's everyday overhead. The skills they bring to your enjoyment are based on years of hard-earned experience, just as your doctor or your lawyer trained for years to help you, and to charge a hefty fee to do it. Those who have a problem with paying a hunting or fishing guide $230.00 a day might try hiring a lawyer, doctor, or for that matter a plumber or electrician for half the time.

I am not, could not, and would not be a professional guide, but I have gotten an inkling of what being a guide entails every time I have taken one person or a few people out hunting or fishing, with the expectation on their part that I am going to lead them to success. Frequently, these happen to be friends who are knowledgeable about various other outdoor pursuits but are depending on me to give them insight into something they aren't experienced with. No money changes hands, it is all in the good fun of companionship (maybe it's the repayment of a similar service on their part sometime in the past), but there is still an undercurrent of responsibility, an unspoken presumption that they can trust in me.

Thus did I find myself, one spring, in charge of a three-hunter expedition (counting myself) to the turkey habitat of the South Platte River bottoms on the plains of northeastern Colorado. There, Colorado Division of Wildlife game managers have established transplants of Rio Grande turkeys to the narrow, brushy, cottonwood-lined corridor of the river between roughly Greeley,

Colorado, on the west and the Nebraska line on the east. Where no turkeys existed twenty years ago (although the native Merriam's subspecies always have been relatively abundant elsewhere in the state), some fifteen hundred of the non-native Rio Grandes now thrive along the winding river.

Paul Wallace, George Uyeno, and I had gotten lucky enough to each draw one of the limited spring permits for a unit in the Fort Morgan-to-Sterling strip of the river. Paul, though a veteran bird hunter, had never hunted turkeys, and George, an accomplished elder statesman among Colorado outdoor sportsmen, had been skunked the few times he had tried it. Neither knew much about how to call gobblers in the spring.

This was early in the history of limited-permit hunting of river-dwelling Rio Grandes in Colorado. Hunting pressure was still light, and these turkeys hadn't had time to get wary of voluble hens that they somehow couldn't see.

"I think we'll do pretty well," I babbled, in what is as close to an ironclad, mortal-lock guarantee as I'm ever likely to make in my unofficial guiding capacities. I really do know better.

On the second day of our hunt it was beginning to look like it might be time to cultivate my taste for crow, not turkey. We had been fortunate enough to get permission to use a very well appointed duck-hunting-club lodge on private land as our camp headquarters, complete with kitchen, deck, fireplace, and beds with firm mattreses. But after arriving about noon we went out and hunted the club property all afternoon and found no signs of turkeys except some old tracks in the sand along the riverbed. It was apparent that however great this property might be for ducks, it was poor turkey habitat because it had been leased out for cattle grazing. The cattle had eaten away at the grassy cover on each side of the river, munching it down to the near-bald consistency of a closely manicured golf green. No turkey worth its wattles would spend much time in this neat, coverless park where a predator could see forever.

So we moved the next morning to a Colorado Division of Wildlife public area about 5 miles east. There, the cows had been kept out and the cover was much better, but we still neither heard nor saw a single gobbler or hen. I checked the sign-out register at the parking area and determined that this property had experienced a lot of human traffic over the recent weekend.

I suggested we have some lunch and then spend the afternoon at the next, and larger, state area several miles farther east along the river. I knew it had even thicker cover and generally got hit with less traffic. I was beginning to detect those little sidelong glances that have the unspoken question written all over them: Does this klutz really have a clue what he's talking about? (God love a hunting guide; there is no rule that anybody else has to, at least not until he produces.)

To compound the uneasiness, which was starting to manifest itself in the form of prolonged periods of silence as we drove eastward, the wind had picked up. When the wind blows on the South Platte bottoms—I mean *really* blows—the cottonwood trees literally quake down to their roots. Entire 2-foot-thick trunks and limbs snap off in gale-force winds. It looked like that sort of wind was working itself up.

We parked in the state-designated dirt parking lot a few hundred yards past a farmer's house and decided to split our forces: George would go back west through the trees along the river, and Paul and I would hunt together in an easterly direction. What Paul knew about calling turkeys could be written on a broken-off thumbnail. I would have to do the calling for him.

George's 5-foot-1 Japanese-descent frame (he was then in his midsixties but solid as a rock and fully capable of outwalking a man half his age) faded into the distant trees to the west. Paul and I hoofed it across an open grassy meadow and walked without pausing into the nearest stand of ancient cottonwoods.

The guide had screwed up. I should have suggested that we sit down a short distance into the cover and call for a few minutes.

Instead, we blundered ahead, right into a group of four turkeys.

They looked like gobblers, but I couldn't be sure as their shadowy forms flitted into and out of my vision through the tree trunks and brush 100 yards ahead of us. They were moving at a trot and there was no doubt they had seen us. But they didn't appear to be panicked into full-out flight.

I stopped Paul with a hand on his arm. "Let's just sit here for fifteen minutes or so and give them time to settle down," I said.

There is nothing carved in the bylaws of turkey hunting that says a spooked turkey can't be called back into gun range, despite what our doubts tell us. A gobbler who hears a hunter's hen yelp coming from a place where he saw a man twenty minutes earlier doesn't necessarily associate the sound with humans. If anything, it may be the opposite: If a hen's over there again, he figures, the man must be gone.

Paul and I selected a couple of cottonwood trunks that were abreast of each other and about 8 yards apart. We sat down, pulled up face masks, and waited. After fifteen minutes I stuck the Boss Hen diaphragm in my mouth and cut loose with a long run of lost-hen yelps. I had to really blast them out in between wind gusts, fearing that I wouldn't be heard otherwise. The limbs of the trees creaked, groaned, and swayed above us with each gust of wind.

There was absolutely no answering call from a turkey, and I'm not sure we would have heard it if there had been one. But I looked as far as I could gaze through the tree trunks and low brush and to my delight saw four turkeys walking fast in single file, straight toward our position. They were maybe 100 yards away and closing.

"There they are," I said, as if there had never been a doubt, and waited. I glanced at Paul and saw that he, too, had spotted the birds.

As they closed to 50 yards, I could see their red necks and heads and the dark blotches of their stubby beards. All jakes. They kept coming. I yelped twice more. They stayed true to their course, as silent as woods wraiths. They were not about to yelp or gobble and arouse the ire of any older tom that might be in the vicinity of this lonesome hen they had heard.

The thing about jakes is, you don't know what they're going to do: run to a call, run from it, stand there in a stupefied position of immobility and just listen to it, or sing a chorus of "Fly Me to the Moon." A single jake who has had his butt bounced by a bigger gobbler isn't likely to come to a call. But four of them together seem to have a gang-style bravado, a collective sense of security.

"They're all gobblers," I whispered to my partner, to let him know he didn't have to worry about shooting a hen.

These young toms kept walking, with no hesitancy, down a vague narrow trail through the brush and trees in perfect single file, like soldiers lining up at the payday window. The problem for us was that if they didn't spread out, one shot, not to mention two shots, could kill not only the turkey the shot was intended for, but one or two more to boot.

I whispered to Paul, who had his gun mounted on one knee and was looking down the barrel: "Wait."

At what we later paced off was a distance of 23 yards, the single file of toms came through a narrow place in the trail and decided to spread out broadside. They seemed uncertain about what they had heard, or at least about precisely where it was originating. I hadn't called again. But they knew, as all turkeys know, the approximate, if not the exact, location from which the hen sounds had come. As each young tom widened the distance from his near neighbor, I realized that at this short range the spaces between them were now wide enough that we could avoid hitting a bird by accident when aiming at another one. The shot pattern wouldn't have that much time to spread. I whispered, "I'll take the one on the left." Four red heads popped up in unison.

At the boom of my gun, the gobbler on the left was bowled over, and a half second later Paul's gun sounded and the one on the far right went tumbling down. The two in the middle took off, one flying, the other running.

These, as we discovered after walking up to claim our prizes, were plump 15- to 16-pound toms with beards averaging about 4 inches long. In fact, my tom had a double beard, the only one with two beards I have ever taken, and he had a state division of wildlife band on his leg. I had a momentary feeling of regret that I, or someone else, wouldn't have the opportunity to hunt him and take him two or three years later, in the fullness of his maturity. I learned later, with a telephone call, that he had been among two dozen turkeys trapped three months earlier about 5 miles away. He had been released in the same spot, but most of the others had been transplanted to another location much farther west on the river, to extend the stocking program.

After whooping it up and hand-slapping for a semicivilized interval, Paul and I got around to tagging our young gobblers. It was then that I discovered, in a careful inventory of the contents of my strap-on fanny pack, that it did not contain a pencil or a pen. There was everything else in there that an itinerant turkey hunter (or guide) could possibly need, but no writing implement to sign turkey tags.

My "client," my charge, my pupil, looked at me for deliverance. He didn't have a pen or a pencil either. We had three choices: Don't tag the toms until we got back to the vehicle and retrieved a writing implement; tag them now with no signatures on the tags; or have one guy go to the truck for a pen and leave the other one standing there in the woods with two untagged turkeys. Whichever we chose, we would be temporarily illegal.

It was time for the all-knowing guide to figure something out. Which, in a stroke of masterful improvisation, I did: We each took a twig off the ground and whittled it down to a sharp point with a pocket knife. Then we touched a match (I did have those in my pack) to the pointed end of the twig and burned it. Voilà! A charcoal writing instrument. I hoped that my fledgling turkey hunter was impressed.

We then hoisted the gobblers over our shoulders and headed

back to the parking area to wait for George. The previously agreed upon rendezvous time was 6:00 P.M. It was 5:30.

Gazing toward the river, leaning against the car and sipping beers, we saw him emerge from the distant trees, turkeyless. He stopped suddenly and seemed to be staring down the tree line to the east. Then he resumed his short-legged stride (it eats up ground at a surprising pace) and in a few minutes joined us.

After some ribbing back and forth, George congratulated us and we asked him what he had been looking at when he came out of the trees.

"I saw a turkey on the edge of the trees about 200 yards away, but I didn't know whether I ought to go after it, or what."

"What did the turkey do?"

"Ran back into the trees."

"George," I said, "let's go see if it was a gobbler. It probably was. Let's see if we can call him in. We'll give it twenty minutes." The late-afternoon sun was slanting low through the trees and the wind gusted as fiercely as ever.

George looked at me quizzically, and he told me later that in the wind and in his hearing-impaired condition (he is virtually deaf in one ear) he had thought I said, "We'll get him in twenty minutes." That's a confident guide if ever there was one, or at least George thought so at that moment.

While Paul waited at the vehicle, George and I reentered the trees and I picked a spot to set up and call. Blaring out the Boss Hen, I detected no turkey sound in reply. Because of the wind, I knew we had to change calling positions frequently with steady forward-progress movement in the direction the turkey had gone.

In the third spot we picked I yelped as loud as I could, in a five-yelp series. At one point I thought I heard a turkey cluck, but in the wind it may have been wishful thinking. A few minutes later I looked over to see my partner wiggling and shifting his weight up against the tree trunk behind him, as if trying to scratch his back.

I was about to suggest he quit doing it when he brought his 12 gauge up to firing position.

"I see a turkey," he whispered.

I could see nothing. I asked the obvious question: "Does it have a red head?"

"Huh?"

I realized I was on his deaf side. But George's hawklike eyesight had ascertained what I, with my advantage in hearing, could not: A lone turkey had come silently to the calls, and although I knew a lone bird drawn to calls at this time of year was quite probably a gobbler, I repeated the question as forcefully as a man can while trying to whisper over the wind.

"Yeah," George whispered back. "It's a big one. Should I shoot?"

I took a deep breath. Trying to communicate further on George's deaf side might result in spooking the bird. I had to trust that my partner knew the difference between a hen and a gobbler. So I whispered, "Yeah." And held my breath.

Click.

I couldn't believe it. George, obviously, had forgotten to load his gun.

Boom!

Thoroughly confused now, I scrambled to my feet and followed George to a spot 30 yards away, where, behind brush cover that had been between me and the bird, flopped a magnificent three- or four-year-old Rio Grande gobbler. It had long curved spurs and a beard just past 10 inches.

"What in the hell happened before you shot?" I asked.

"Huh?"

"Your gun just clicked. Did you have a bad shell?" George was shooting an over-under double gun and it was conceivable that the first shell misfired.

George grinned. "Oh. Nah, I'm using a trap gun. It has a release trigger."

Deciding to inquire later why he would select a release-trigger trap gun—pulling the trigger cocks the gun for firing and releasing it causes it to fire—for a turkey hunt, I looked at my watch. Exactly twenty-two minutes had passed since we had left the parking lot in pursuit of this tom, and the sun was now sinking below the horizon. We learned later that George's gobbler would have made it easily into the top ten of the Rio Grande gobbler world rankings of the National Wild Turkey Federation, if he had chosen to enter it. (He did not. George is not one for gilding lilies.)

Back at the duck club, we hung the three gobblers from a tree limb near the front deck. There was much jubilation, along with a round or two of celebratory libations, followed by the guide's rendition of a supper of canned-salmon croquettes with corn and tossed salad. My fledglings praised my guiding skills. They even found something nice to say about the slightly burned croquettes.

"Thank you. Just leave the tips on the table," I said, shuffling off in the direction of the bed.

On my way out of the room, I could have sworn I heard two bucks snort. I never did ask any further questions about the release trigger on George's gun. A smart guide knows that it's better to let some things lie.

12

HEN PARTY

STATE GAME AND FISH AGENCIES, which of necessity must schedule hunting-season dates long before they know variables such as what the weather will be like or (in the case of spring-season turkeys) overwinter survival of the birds, try to do their best to make these seasons productive for the hunter. Some states are so rich in turkeys they can afford to set long seasons that pretty much cover the weather and breeding-period possibilities. But others must try to bracket what is generally referred to as the peak gobbling period.

Most turkey biologists will tell you that there are two main gobbling periods. In the early stage, toms, their reproductive urges responding to the steadily increasing periods of daylight as winter ends and spring begins, begin to look for hens with which to breed. They are in effect gathering harems. The peak stage comes after hens are impregnated and begin to go to nest. The onset of incubation by hens tends to leave gobblers off by themselves for considerable portions of the day, meaning that they are more likely to gobble to attract company. In between these two stages there may not be much gobbling.

So, theoretically, the hunter is less likely to encounter the problem of gobblers surrounded by hens in the last half of, say, a month-long season, than he is in the first half. But if the hunter waits too long and the season extends late into the spring, he may find himself stuck in the worst of all possible spring-turkey-hunting worlds: Breeding is essentially over and almost all gobbling has ceased.

All of this sounds pretty cut-and-dried on paper. But paper is one thing and the real turkey season is something else. Most experienced turkey hunters have learned that gobblers may be hanging out with groups of hens, or vice versa, at any time of the season. For whatever reasons—wet weather, cold weather, dry weather, a late spring, an early spring—nesting may come earlier or later in a given spring in a given area than it normally does.

The upshot is that hens can be a complication in any spring hunt at any stage of the season, and this is such a common factor that many of us have taken to using it as the one ironclad excuse for not bagging a bird: "Yeah, I saw plenty of gobblers, but they all had hens with them." Meaning, of course, that the toms had no reason to come to a call—they already had their datebooks full. The other hunters to whom you are telling this tale of woe nod in sympathy. They have been there, and they have used this same explanation for coming up empty. It's always handy, like a pot of coffee simmering for unexpected guests.

What we conveniently overlook when we give up on hen-surrounded gobblers, or use it as an excuse, is that turkeys are gregarious birds. They have a strong flocking instinct. (There are exceptions, of course. The so-called hermit gobblers, for instance, who spend the bulk of their lives in lofty, suspicious isolation. Or the pal-around older gobblers who stick together in small bunches through the fall and winter and who seem to view other turkeys the way the Mafia views undercover cops.)

Although gobblers are drawn to hens in the spring, hens are drawn not just to gobblers but to other hens. Turkeys also have pecking orders and territorial jealousies. Finally, hens have protective, motherly, matronly-boss, busybody characteristics. For all these reasons, hens are often drawn to the yelps or cutts of other hens or the yelps of young gobblers.

What the spring gobbler hunter must do when confronted with a mature tom that refuses to leave the company of a hen or group of hens is forget the gobbler, at least for a while. Stop thinking in terms of calling in the tom and start thinking in terms of what it takes to call in the hen or hens. Because, generally speaking, it's this simple: If the hens move somewhere, the tom is going to move with them.

We are often discouraged when we locate a gobbler or gobblers and then hear the sound of hen yelps in the same vicinity. We will have good reason to be disheartened if the hens don't move toward us. The idea is to get them to do that, and the way to start is to stir up their interest with persistent yelps or impertinent cutting or cackling.

On a hunt in Kansas one spring, I almost gave up on a couple of toms and their hens after they flew down from the roost and went in the opposite direction from me. But not having another plan to fall back on, I decided to follow through the trees at a discreet distance. The flock eventually ended up out in the open, in a wheat-stubble field about 50 yards from the edge of the trees.

I sat a few yards back in the trees and brush and yelped. The gobblers answered occasionally, but they were the kind of answers you get when a tom is simply making sure other turkeys in the area know his territory.

After a long while I was about to consider moving somewhere else when it dawned on me that with a certain pitch and tone of yelp with one of my mouth callers, I was getting some answering yelps from at least a couple of hens. This went on for some time, to the point where I figured the conversation was never going to progress out of the long-distance stage. But then three of the hens started moving back toward the trees, still answering, and within five minutes they came walking down a farmer's tractor road separating the field from the trees, trailed by one of the toms. I shut up and let the slightly confused hens go past and the tom came abreast of me, 20 yards away. I downed him right there in the road.

I have sat on the edge of similar clearings for up to two hours watching a mixed bunch of turkeys drift around in an apparently random feeding pattern while I called, when it dawned on me that, little by little, they were closing the distance between us. Sometimes, they came all the way, sometimes they didn't. But whatever response I induced could be attributed to the hens, not the gobblers.

One mistake a hunter can easily make in the classic roost-trees-at-dawn situation is waiting too long to call when hens are roosted in the near vicinity of a gobbler or gobblers. I am generally a believer in the theory that it doesn't pay to start yelping too soon, when it's still too dark for turkeys to be on the ground. This may arouse the suspicions of a gobbler. I feel a little foolish tree-clucking or yelping from a spot on the ground when all the hens in the vicinity are still on their roost limbs. Surely, I figure, the tom won't believe that a hen is roosted 3 feet off the ground in a clump of brush.

But I have been caught while coolly (I thought) waiting until the last minute. Hens are yelping from somewhere on the other side of the roosted gobbler, and suddenly, seemingly far too early, the gobbler flies down. He is flying down because he has heard the hens in the other direction and is eager to get close enough to them to attract their attention by strutting or gobbling, or both. I frantically begin yelping when this happens, only to find on most occasions that the tom will keep going toward the hens he heard first. Probably the best approach when a hunter hears yelps from roosted hens is to immediately try to outyelp them, either attracting the hens themselves or sounding more sexy to the gobbler than the real ones.

The term "Boss Hen" is more than just a cute marketing gimmick for somebody who sells turkey yelpers. There tend to be, I am convinced, older hens in a drove of turkeys that more or less are in charge of where and what the drove does. Appeal to the motherly or combative instincts of this hen and the other turkeys are likely to follow her lead.

I am reminded of the time I was on a whitetail hunt in the hill country of central Texas. Turkeys were the last thing on my mind, but I and another hunter were sitting in a ground blind late one afternoon, hoping to see a big buck emerge from the brush, when we heard the muted yelps of a drove of approaching Rio Grande turkeys. I turned slowly to see that the flock was headed more or less directly toward the blind from behind us. There probably were thirty to forty turkeys in this bunch, mixed hens, poults, and a few gobblers.

When the flock got to a point about 60 yards from us, a single large hen separated herself from the rest and walked slowly, quietly, but resolutely up to the blind. We held our collective breath just to see what this bird was going to do.

So help me, she walked around to an opening in the blind, peered in, saw us, jerked her head straight up and putted as loudly as I have ever heard a turkey putt. Whereupon the flock began to run back in the direction it had come, and the boss hen followed after them.

Now that, friends, is a pretty sharp turkey, gobbler or not. It appeared exactly as if she had appointed herself to go over and see if the men-creatures she had seen before in this strange box happened to be in it this particular evening.

If you can fool that kind of a turkey, the gobblers will fall into place.

13

A Gobbler to Crow About

My partner lay encased in his sleeping bag, mummy-like, and the bag shook like one of those vibrator beds in a cheap motel room. His fever had to be somewhere at the 102-degree level or worse; we didn't know, because we didn't have a thermometer. Doug was lying on his makeshift wooden-platform bunk built against one of the walls of the old mine-processing shed.

Finally he crawled out of the bag, got dressed, shakily donned a jacket, and began gathering up his stuff. "If I'm going to die," he said, "I'm going to do it in the comfort of my own bed."

He assured me he was physically able to drive himself to that bed, about 85 miles away. The last I saw of him through the lightly falling rain, he was driving his pickup out of sight around the bend in the muddy road. Doug had contracted some sort of bug on this spring hunt. Luckily, the fever and chills hadn't set in until after he had killed his gobbler during a brief break in what so far had been a siege of dismal, unseasonably cold weather.

I stayed alone in camp. I had the rest of this afternoon, all day tomorrow, and half the day after that left to hunt before I would have to pack up and head back to Denver. Nothing much, except Doug bagging his tom, had gone smoothly on this hunt. It had been drizzling and sleeting when we drove into our hunting area, fishtailing the two vehicles down the slick roads in four-wheel-drive like a couple of wild stock-car drivers in a demolition derby. In the subsequent two days the weather had warmed somewhat, but dry periods of sunshine only intermittently broke up a gray, wet overcast.

That night, after sitting out most of the afternoon rain in camp, I found myself heating up some stew in all but total darkness by the light of a flashlight. The lantern batteries had pooped out and I didn't have any replacements. There isn't a hell of a lot to do for entertainment with no lights at night in a one-man hunting camp, so I crawled into the sack after the meal and went to sleep.

I had drawn up a game plan for the morning. During the brief time I had been out the afternoon before, I had blundered along in the light rain and spooked three gobblers feeding right out in the middle of a pasture near the east fork of the creek. They had flown in the direction of the greening-out cottonwood roost trees farther up the narrow little creek-bottom canyon. I did not follow them. I knew if they settled down in that area, one or more of them would roost near where I last saw them.

So, as I waited for dawn the next morning, I did so under the semiprotective umbrella of a juniper tree and faced in the direction of the creekside cottonwoods about 100 yards distant. The light rain was falling again, and a miniwaterfall found its way down through the juniper branches and culminated in a trickle down the inside back of my camo rain jacket. I shivered, wondering if I was merely cold and wet or whether I was coming down with whatever had made Doug sick.

The sun did not rise. Instead, its subdued light very gradually began to permeate the gray atmosphere from all directions at once. I had heard nothing and decided to owl-hoot.

A gobbler answered from a cottonwood tree no more than 120 yards away. I shivered again, but this time I did it with a smile on my face. I switched to a mouth yelper (one of the handier aspects of a mouth diaphragm is that you don't have to worry about getting it wet) and gave the tom a few tentative tree clucks. He answered, but not immediately. That was the first clue that I might be in a bit of trouble. Truly hot gobblers answer back immediately.

I know a guy who, early in the telling of a hunting or fishing story, always says, "To make a long story short . . ." So, to make a long story short, the tom flew down, but not in my direction. I could hear him occasionally gobble in sort of a halfhearted way as I desperately tried to tempt him into a U-turn. No dice. I decided to follow a safe distance behind. He was on the other side of the little creek and walking northward, upcanyon. I could follow without detection by creeping along, using the creekside banks and growth for cover. The creek itself was only a trickle and it was easy to stay in the streambed.

This tom was playing hard to get, and when I saw him for the first time I understood why: He was strolling along in the company of a comely hen, and he obviously wasn't the insatiable polygamist type—one lady friend at a time was plenty for him.

Just for the education of it, I trailed along out of sight, watching the two birds, who were gradually increasing the distance between us. At that point, a noisy crow flew over. The crow cawed loudly just as it reached a point almost directly over the gobbler's head, and the tom stopped, stretched out his neck, and gobbled fiercely. He did this not once but three times as the rest of a busy-body flock of vocal crows crisscrossed the air space over the turkeys' heads.

The crows had elicited more passion from the tom than my hen yelps had. He obviously had no great affection for crows, and I wondered yet again what it is about owls and crows, other than the intrusive noises they make, that so excites, or irritates, some gobblers.

This study in turkey behavior, as fascinating as it was, did me no practical good for the rest of the day, and I ended it sitting for-lornly and damply at the perimeter of another roost area, where I observed absolutely nothing with feathers going to bed for the night. Maybe the rain-spattered gobblers had just crawled under a bush and said the hell with it. If so, I couldn't blame them.

Later, supper by flashlight was anything but romantic in the tin-roofed shed. I took comfort from a 90 proof dose of Kentucky's finest elixir and crawled into the dry warmth of the sleeping bag.

This shed had a round, pie-piece-partitioned sorting bin underneath a flumelike funnel that came down from above the roof. Rain trickled down it and dripped into the bin. Obviously it was some sort of ore-processing rig, but it looked decidedly Rube Goldbergish to me. I once asked Doug the history of this strange building, sitting as it did in the heart of ranch country, and he told me that someone had set up what was supposed to be a copper-mining operation here in the wilds of southeastern Colorado. I doubted that southeastern Colorado had a reputation as a mother lode of copper ore, but apparently that hadn't occurred to the gullible investors who blew their money on this scheme. No cop-per of any significance was found, and the shed stood as a monu-ment to scams fueled by get-rich-quick dreams. (A few years later we were to learn that the shed, actually big enough to be a barn, had been torn down over the winter. I asked why, and Doug said the owners wanted to be shed, pardon the pun, of the two hundred dollars a year in property taxes they paid to the county. Standing, the shed was a two-hundred-dollar-a-year liability in renderings unto Caesar; torn down into a pile of junk lumber and metal, it was technically and legally worth nothing. Certainly it was no longer worth anything to us. Both Doug and I would have been willing to pay the tax just to continue using it as a camp headquarters, but such is the paradox of the tax laws.)

I decided to play my last hand out at the same roost area where I had watched the gobbler who hated crows. I walked in the darkness before dawn to the same juniper. The ground was still sodden, but overnight the sky had cleared totally in that wonderful Western way that signals the arrival of a dominating high-pressure ridge that seems to say, "Okay, enough of this dismal shit, let's get back to paradise."

An hour of calling on what would seem to be a perfect morning for gobbling produced not a single responding turkey sound. I thought of Tom Kelly's observation in his book, *Tenth Legion,* that a hunter could go out the next morning after a previous day of hearing the woods come alive with gobbles, stand in the same tracks he made the day before under the same barometric conditions, and hear absolutely nothing. If anything, the conditions this day were better than the day before, but if a turkey was roosted in my area, he wasn't inclined to let anybody or anything know about it.

I am not a steadfast believer in what might as well be called "the last-cast theory." That somehow, if you make one more cast (or cover one more field or one more ridge on a hunting trip), you are necessarily going to be rewarded with the fish or the bird or the deer or whatever turns the whole venture around. Often, the fabled sundown spurt of action on a fishing or hunting trip never materializes, and you are left to curse the *Solunar Tables* and whoever propounded the dogma that the last hour of the day is worth all the rest put together. This sometimes proves to be true in such endeavors as walleye fishing or dove shooting or deer hunting, but it is no more etched in granite than a politician's campaign promises.

I am a believer, however, in the practicality that you aren't going to catch any fish or bag any game if you are back in camp, or on your way home. To the extent that there is any time left on a so-far-unproductive hunting or fishing trip, I usually try to use it, and then pack it in when that time comes, but not before.

So I began a circling sweep of the terrain surrounding the creek, calling for twenty minutes or so in a spot, then moving a few hundred yards and doing it again. In the ensuing three hours I found tracks and other signs that turkeys were using the area (which I already knew, anyway) but neither heard nor saw a gobbler or hen.

By 11 A.M. it was time to head back to the parked vehicle and drive back to break camp and head home. I knew that in the late stages of the season, chances of finding a hot, henless gobbler in the midday hours are always good. But time for me was running out, and I wore disconsolate thoughts around my neck like the prover-bial albatross as I plodded down the two-track four-wheel-drive trail that led to the Bronco. As rewarding as any turkey hunt is, there is a ponderous letdown when you come to the end of it with-out a gobbler in an area you know holds plenty of them.

I reached a point where I could stay in the rut road and circle around the base of a rocky finger ridge while remaining on flat ground, the easiest and quickest way to the vehicle. It was tempting to do that, because I was tired. Or, I could take a straight shot up the ridge through the rocks and the junipers and get to the base of the rimrock mesa, where, before descending the other side, I would be able to send out some loud yelps that could be heard both up on top of the rim and for considerable distances below. Some sort of voice was saying, "Walk up that ridge and call one more time."

The ridge became much steeper than it looked as I worked my way uphill, periodically pausing to give city-softened legs and overtaxed lungs a break. About two-thirds of the way to the rim I stopped again. At that precise moment, a crow flew over and cawed.

A gobble shattered the stillness after the caw.

I held my breath, listening. The crow cawed once more, and the tom gobbled again. He sounded as if he were no more than 100 yards ahead of me, on my level, out of sight in the boulders and scrubby trees. I could hardly believe this eleventh-hour stroke of good fortune, and I had no doubt that this was my crow-hating gobbler. The crow had saved me from blundering right into the tom and spooking him.

The question was this: Was he with a hen (or hens) again, or was he alone?

Because of the time of day, chances of the latter were good. Hens for the most part had gone to nest by now, leaving still-amorous toms wandering in search of company. This is a fact of spring turkey hunting that seems to escape many hunters, who think that if they don't score in the early hours, the game is over for the day. Actually, their chances of calling in a tom, if they can find one, increase considerably in the middle hours of the day. You may see or hear more toms around roost areas at dawn, but your percentage of success in calling them in will be lower than for individual toms traveling at midday without hens.

Hurriedly, I sat down with my back against a big rock. The view out in front of me was blocked in the center by a bigger boulder about 15 yards away, leaving possible shooting lanes on either side. It was not an ideal place to set up, but judging by how near the gobbler was, it would have to do. On the other hand, the turkey would not be able to see me until he emerged on either side of the boulder.

I slipped the box caller out of my pack and stroked it four times. The tom gobbled back instantly, and at that moment I knew he was alone. I waited two or three minutes, then yelped again, and got an answer again. The gobbler sounded much closer than he had the first time.

I put the box down beside me and tried to forget it was there. The tom had answered, he was on his way, and he knew almost exactly where I was. Sometimes I think it must have been a wild turkey that invented the global-positioning systems that allow anglers, hunters, boaters, and others to program their way to a precise spot on land or water. Further calling would only serve to convince this tom that the hen he had heard was so eager that she would meet him halfway.

The tom gobbled again. The Bird of Paradise (or would it be Purgatory?) was now almost within gun range, somewhere out of sight beyond that boulder in front of me. The rock I sat against was beginning to feel like a dull knife buried in my spinal column. Minutes passed as if they were hours. The tom didn't gobble again, but every instinct in my hunter's makeup, every piece of turkey-hunting experience stored away in my subsconscious mind, told me he was there.

I stared to the right of the boulder. Nothing. I stared to the left. Still nothing. Risking detection, I gambled: I very, very slowly and carefully scooted my butt to the left, all the time holding the gun ready over one knee, my back scraping silently against the rock. I had to be able to see more space on one or the other side of the boulder, and I really don't know what moved me to choose the left side.

As it turned out, I had to move no more than a foot to see the tom, standing there about 30 yards away, just past the boulder, on the edge of a little drop-off shelf that overlooked the slope leading down to the base of the ridge.

The tom was looking downhill, staring fixedly in that direction. Just in the split second before I fired, I wondered what he could be looking at, or whether he simply was trying to find the hen he knew was somewhere close.

The tom did a flip-flop and bounced over the ledge, tumbling down the rock-strewn slope. I jumped up and moved as fast as my cramped muscles would allow, ready to fire again if necessary. It wasn't necessary.

I made my way down to the gobbler, a mature tom with an 8-inch beard. At this particular rain-soaked, misfortune-dogged cotillion, the last dance had proved to be the best one of all. Or last cast, if you prefer. The fat lady had sung rather late, but as Yogi Berra is supposed to have said, "It ain't over 'til it's over."

As I stood looking at the bird, and then gazing out over a valley sparkling in the sunlight of a pure spring day in Western turkey country, I saw what the gobbler had been staring at: A hundred yards below, its white roof glaring with reflection in the bright midday sun, was my parked Bronco.

Paradise had been closer than I thought.

14

By George

ONE OF THE PERKS OF BEING a writer on hunting and fishing subjects, or for that matter being a hunter or angler whether you write about it or not, is the people you meet. Some trips are more memorable for the personalities you shared them with than for what happened with the fish or the game.

Somehow, one way or another, a trip with George Uyeno, a patriarch of Colorado outdoorsmen, is always memorable. George, as this is written, has passed his seventy-fifth birthday, and he keeps racking up these life-span annuities with the nonchalance of a man plucking grapes off a stem. He hasn't slowed down yet, as near as his friends can tell. If anything, he has speeded up since his retirement from the shoe- and wader-repair business he owned for many years on lower Broadway near downtown Denver. He continues to hone his long-cultivated outdoor skills, and he has plenty of time to develop some new ones, such as he did when he took up spring turkey hunting about ten years ago.

Running the repair shop cramped his style a bit as an outdoorsman, but only in the sense that some days had to be spent at work instead of in the outdoors. The shop was a kind of halfway house for wayward fishermen and hunters. Just about any afternoon, two or three guys with idle time on their hands would drop in, gather in the back of the shop with George amidst the machinery and the worn-down loafers, the hole-in-the-sole boots, and the broken-heeled ladies' pumps and swap stories, information, lies, lures, and fly patterns. George would keep up his end of the conversation while working with the leather, rubber, and canvas. More used reels and guns were sold or traded there, probably, than at any flea market in the state.

The business George ran wasn't high-tech or sophisticated, nor did it offer same-day service. It simply got the job done. It was the only shop in town specializing in wader repair. George had an old 1930s-vintage bathtub in the basement, which he kept filled with water for whenever a customer brought in a pair of leaky chest waders or hip boots. He would take an air hose and fill up the waders, clamp them off, and then dunk them under the surface to see where the air bubbles were coming from.

Sometimes, those of us who hung around the shop felt empathy for customers who came in at the wrong time to drop something off or pick up a repaired pair of shoes or waders. If the hot-stove league was in a critical inning and the conversation was getting really interesting, George was half irritated when the little bell on the front door would tinkle and he had to get up and wait on the customer: "What kind of shoes were they? What color, did you say?" George often forgot to put the claim check number on a repaired pair and a lengthy search would ensue while the shoes' owner became increasing apprehensive. Somehow, though, the elusive shoes always turned up. They were always fixed, and probably were in a more durable condition than when they were new.

When Uyeno retired, like Satchel Paige, he never looked back. If anything was gaining on George Uyeno, it would have to pick up the pace. George, with his wife, Dora, or any of his several regular outdoor companions, began to fish or hunt somewhere almost daily, depending on the season and the weather.

George is perfectly qualified, physically and mentally, for the job of being a retired outdoor-sporting gentleman. Blocky and very short, his Japanese frame reminds you of a midget sumo wrestler with considerably more muscle than fat. Eternally stoic, he walks or wades or casts until he has the day and the quarry figured out. If he comes up empty, he seeks information from his extensive network of pals and informants and returns another day to reverse the outcome. He takes much of what he hears with a grain of salt but forgets nothing if it has the ring of truth, or even the hint of possibility, to it. At one time he held the Colorado record for walleye and he would have held the Wyoming record for ohrid trout (a European import), but the day he caught the fish in the North Platte River he thought it was just an odd-looking brown trout. The true identification was made later from a photo.

George is generous to a fault. More than one mentally, physically, or financially handicapped angler owes some of his happier days on the water to George's willingness to pick needy friends up, pay their way, and return them back home again.

The Uyeno physical tenacity owes in part to a lifetime of abstinence from such vices as tobacco and alcohol. On a couple of occasions, a few of us talked him into having a celebratory drink or two on a particularly rewarding hunt, only to discover that three things are bound to happen: George starts telling stories very fast, he begins to sweat, and the whites of his eyes go bloodshot. We have concluded that he is allergic to booze, a malady some of his friends certainly cannot claim (at least not until the morning after).

The Uyeno physical and emotional resiliency can be traced to good genetics, the pristine life of a farm boy growing up in California, and to the sad days in this country when the U.S. government incarcerated citizens of Japanese descent during World War II. George never talks of those days and there is no indication that he holds the slightest grudge about them. He doesn't think of himself as Japanese, he thinks of himself as American, and I once heard him make a remark about something "the Japs" were doing with foreign trade. I was taken aback until I realized that, in his mind, he was referring to a foreign country, not to a race that he in fact is a member of.

Once, when we were hunting a new (to us) turkey area on a large public wildlife tract in western Oklahoma, George got turned around (he might even admit he was, in fact, lost) in unfamiliar terrain and found himself walking 8 miles in 90-degree heat before he found his way back to camp. Somewhere along the way he came across an isolated farmhouse.

Having long since run out of water, and dehydrated to the point of exhaustion, George knocked on the door and asked for a drink of water. He could see a garden hose hooked up in the yard.

A very nervous-looking woman came to the door, took one look at this shotgun-carrying, camo-clad, Asian, military-looking intruder, and must have concluded that World War II had started again. Or that George was a saboteur who had been out there in the woods all this time without getting the word about the surrender. "We have to bring all our water in," she lied. "Sorry."

George merely grimaced, thanked her politely anyway, turned around, and resumed his march. We found him staggering along a trail a half mile from camp. He drank three cans of Pepsi so fast I thought he was going to choke. I wanted to go back and choke some sense into the farm woman.

As mentioned in an earlier chapter describing a spring hunt with George, he is hard of hearing. Almost stone deaf on one side, in fact. It had to do with a childhood illness, but no doubt decades of firing guns or being around guns that were being fired, as well as noisy shoe-repair machinery, didn't help.

Poor hearing is not an insignificant handicap on a spring turkey hunt. The ability to detect gobbles (sometimes faint and far away) in answer to hen yelps, for instance, may mean the difference between success and an unused turkey tag.

But George offsets it with his incredible eyesight. He has never worn glasses. On a cross-country highway trip he usually is the one who spots the odd hawk, or the distant antelope, or the cock pheasant, or the rare peregrine falcon.

It sort of becomes a game of one-upmanship. You try to beat George to the roadside attraction. Once, a partner of George's pulled the ultimate "gotcha." While George was gazing off to one side of the highway for some sign of wildlife, the vehicle went by a farmhouse on the other side, and in the back of the house there was tethered, for some crazy reason, an elephant. The guy with George triumphantly announced, "George, you missed the elephant."

The hearing problem makes for some humorous situations, although that's easy for those of us without hearing problems to say. I'm sure it's much less amusing to George. Once, George and I were camped in his van along the South Platte River bottoms, each holding a permit to hunt Rio Grande turkeys. We had to camp in an established state campground, but there were no turkeys in the immediate vicinity. We made plans to drive in the morning about 15 miles downriver to a state wildlife area and to be set up to hunt well before dawn.

We miscalculated the time of the next day's sunrise. When we pulled into the wildlife area parking lot the eastern sky already was pale, and in less than 15 minutes it would be turkey fly-down time.

As I hurriedly gathered my gun and gear inside the van, George, as usual one step ahead of me, went outside to wait. Sitting there sorting out shells and calling devices and cramming them into a fanny pack, I heard a surprisingly loud gobble from someplace very close. What the hell was George doing practicing gobble calls at this hour, I wondered.

I stepped out the door of the van and said, "George, did you just give a gobble call?" That was the easiest explanation I could think of. Gobblers don't usually roost in parking lots.

"Huh?"

"Gobble," I repeated. "Did you hear a gobble, or did *you* gobble?"

"No, I didn't hear anything," he said, looking puzzled.

Just then the gobbler cut loose again. Incredibly, the tom was roosted just across the blacktop road from the parking lot in a cottonwood tree growing right alongside the road. His roost limb overlooked the road and we had driven almost directly underneath it just before we pulled into the parking lot. George's eyes got wider and I knew he had finally picked up the sound of the gobbling tom. He was facing away from the tree, looking at me. "What was that?" he asked.

I shook my head in amazement. We could probably crawl up and shoot the roosted gobbler off his limb if we were so inclined, which of course we weren't. I was shaking my head again an hour later when, after we tried to sneak away from the van and get into calling position by making a long, circuitous approach to the backside of this parking-lot roost tree, it became apparent that the gobbler had flown down while we were moving. He was no longer in the tree, or anywhere else nearby. At least we didn't have far to go to get back to the van.

Once, in Wyoming, George and another hunter were visiting with the rancher on whose land they were hunting spring gobblers. They were sitting at a dining room table sipping coffee, when somebody noticed a faint, high-pitched beeping sound permeating the room. To nobody's surprise, George said, "I don't hear anything."

The rancher looked baffled, and a search ensued to determine whether aliens had landed or some militant revolutionary had planted a time bomb. After five minutes of tracking the sound, somebody discovered that George had left his hearing aid turned on in the pocket of his hunting jacket, which was draped over a nearby chair. The hearing aid was emitting the beeping noise.

George, in an outdoor sense, is a Renaissance man. He was a spin fisherman for decades, and it wasn't until his sixties that he decided to check out all this hype about fly fishing. Often he had used large streamer flies below lead weights on spinning line to take big river-dwelling browns and rainbows, but he didn't own a fly rod. He decided to make the leap (and this was well before Robert Redford got so many fly-fishing wannabes all fired up over a film based on Norman Maclean's book, *A River Runs Through It*). Three years after taking up fly fishing, George owned three graphite rods and was tying his own flies, matching the hatches with the best of us. The spinning tackle now gathers dust most of the year.

He brought the same intensity, fascination, and dedication to turkey hunting. He still can't make realistic hen sounds come out of a diaphragm, but he works a kind of methodical artistry with the raspiness of a good slate caller. Most of all, he never quits, not until the sun goes down anyway, and then only temporarily.

One hunt will serve as an example of what I am talking about.

The two of us headed to eastern Wyoming, where we had permission from a sheep rancher to hunt the Merriam's turkeys that inhabit the rugged pine ridges, draws, and canyons that surround the North Platte River and its tributaries.

We arrived at noon after driving three hours through a steadily falling rain. We parked the camper van in the mud near the ranch barns and quickly deduced that we would be unable to drive up the two-track rut road that led from the ranch house 3 miles over a flat-topped ridge to the creek bottom we normally hunted. It would be a crapshoot even for a four-wheel-drive vehicle, which we didn't have.

We hunted the first afternoon on the ridges near the house, seeing old sign but neither hearing (I speak of myself) nor seeing a turkey. The rain came down in a constant drizzle, and our stiff rain gear crackled as we walked. We were sweating under the rainwear, even though the air was cold.

The next day, the rain fell intermittently in the morning, and the gracious rancher offered us the use of his three-wheel all-terrain buggy kept for ranch chores. This man was one of a dwindling breed in Wyoming, an operator of an independent family-controlled ranch where friends and acquaintances are always welcome. We didn't know it then, but a bank had foreclosed on him and he was about to join the ranks of those whose ranches and farms have been lost to corporations or well-heeled out-of-state ownership. It is a sadly familiar refrain in the Western states.

We gratefully accepted the offer of the ATV and took off up the road that would lead us over the top of the ridge and down to the creek on the other side. The rancher's sheepdog trotted along eagerly about 20 feet behind the ATV, ignoring our efforts to stop and coax him back to the house. Evidently he was used to following family members or ranch hands using the ATV around the property.

Dogs are great things to have on most bird hunts, but they make an awkward fit on a turkey safari. I finally convinced the dog to head back to the ranch house when I bounced a small rock off his rear end. His feelings were hurt more than his derriere.

I had a chance that afternoon to shoot one of three jakes that were palling around along the creek bottom but saw nothing of older gobblers except their tracks. I passed on the jakes. George found nothing at all in a hunt uphill through one of the tributary draws—actually small steep-sided canyons bordered by grassy ridges studded with ponderosa pine. (With the typically understated Uyeno-style generosity, he had left me the easier terrain of the creek bottom.)

That's the way it continued through half the next day, our last opportunity, although overnight the rain had quit. Once again we used the ATV to get to our hunting area. By early afternoon I was discouraged and tired and said so. There were still a few hours of possible hunting time before we had to go home, but I suggested to George that we head back to the van, heat up some leftover chili for a late lunch, and then make a decision whether to hit the road or not.

I was driving the ATV and George was sitting behind me when we came over the crest of the dividing ridge between the creek bottom and the valley where the ranch buildings were. Off to our right, steep draws and hollows lined with ponderosa pine angled away to the valley floor.

"Bob, let me off here," George said. "I'll take about an hour and hunt downhill to the ranch. See you at the van."

I started to point out to him that he would be hunting the same unproductive area we had covered the first afternoon, but this was a new day, the sun was out, and George wasn't about to give up without one more shot at the brass ring. I wished him luck. He waddled off and disappeared into the pine trees. I aimed the ATV downhill, grinding in low gear through the residual mud, toward the distant ranch buildings. Neither one of us had so much as heard a gobble on the entire hunt, although it was possible that George, even with his hearing aid turned on, had been near a gobbling tom at some point and not known it.

I rumbled down to the parked van, pulled off my mud-caked boots, and went inside to heat up the chili. I ate a cup of it, popped open a can of beer, and managed to drink half of it before I fell asleep.

I was awakened by the sound of my name. It fit right in with the dream I was having. In the dream, somebody unseen was calling to me across a foggy canyon, somebody trying to tell me where the turkeys were.

In reality, George was coming through the corral gate near the barn, calling out to me, and when I looked out the van window I knew where the turkeys were. One of them, anyway: A huge Merriam's gobbler with a long beard was draped over George's chunky shoulders, its wings drooping outward and weakly flapping with George's stride, creating the effect of some squat-bodied angel about to launch himself into the heavens.

"I heard him gobble," George said excitedly, in a tone of wonderment. The fact that he had heard the gobble seemed to mean more to him than the fact that he had killed the bird. "But I didn't know which direction the sound was coming from."

"What'd you do?"

"I had just sat down against a pine tree. I was stopping to call about every two hundred yards. He gobbled as soon as I used the slate. I waited a little, worked the slate again, and he gobbled right back."

In the confusion that comes with faulty ears, George never did locate the position of the tom by the sound of his gobble. The sound seemed to be descending from all directions at once.

George simply stroked the slate one more time, picked up his gun, and let those eagle eyes take over.

The rest was easy, by George.

15

ASSUME THE POSITION

SOME WISE SALESMAN ORIGINALLY BESTOWED upon us what has become the most hallowed cliché, and a very valuable, practical one, in the realm of real estate: The three most important things to consider about property are "location, location, and location." I don't know who this dealer in frontages, lots, and acreage may have been, but I'm convinced he had the makings of a fine turkey hunter.

Other factors being more or less equal, *where* you are when you sit down to sing your siren song to a lovesick tom is more important than how skillful a caller you happen to be. Years of gobbler-chasing successes and failures, as well as conversations with other hunters, have led me to believe that a mediocre caller in a good spot is far more likely to bag his bird than an expert caller in a poor spot.

There are some routes a gobbler will not take, places he will not go, and obstacles he will not cross. Note that I say "a" gobbler. Each one has the potential to be different. No one can be positive that there isn't a tom turkey who would fly across the Mississippi River from Arkansas to be shot in Tennessee if the hunter calling him was loud and persuasive enough. But the job of the hunter is to make the gobbler's journey as relatively short and easy as possible.

This doesn't mean you have to be within 60 yards of the bird when you start calling to him, although on very windy days you may have to be a lot closer than usual just to be heard. (If I had to pick an average ideal distance from the turkey for calling purposes, it probably would be about 150 to 200 yards.) What it does mean is that you don't want to have something between you and the bird that he doesn't want to cross, fly over, or detour a long distance around.

Many hunters have observed toms that refuse, for example, to go over, under, or through a barbed-wire or woven-wire fence. The sight of a tom standing on the other side of such a fence and irritably gobbling his snood off, as if he were faced with the Great Wall of China, seems somewhat ridiculous, since all the bird has to do is fly about 10 feet. Likewise a tom that will not fly or wade across a narrow creek where the water is barely deep enough to lap over a man's boot tops. This doesn't mean *all* gobblers will slam on the brakes when encountering creeks or fences, but it certainly leads one to believe that it pays to be on his side of the barrier when the calling commences.

The smart caller positions himself so that fences, creeks, rivers, canyons, cactus patches, walls of thick brush or weeds, and major roads, to name some examples, aren't between him and the gobbler.

Dick Kirby, president of Quaker Boy calls and winner of more calling contests than he can remember, confides quite candidly that he believes calling is no more than 40 to 50 percent of the game in gobbler hunting, whereas position is 50 to 60 percent.

"An average caller who has good woodsmanship skills will be more successful than a very good caller who doesn't," says Kirby.

Kirby, who has hunted turkeys all over the United States and Mexico, believes there's a correlation between how easy or difficult it is to call in a tom across potential barriers and how much hunting pressure the turkeys are getting in the area. "I've called them across highways out West, where there's little pressure," he said, "but the sport is growing in the Western states and those birds are beginning to get educated." The more heavily hunted an area, the more picky a gobbler is likely to be in choosing his traveling routes, Kirby is convinced.

One accepted rule of thumb in turkey hunting is that it's difficult to call a tom downhill from the bird's position. "Your first choice is to be slightly above the turkey, your second choice is to be on his level, and your last choice is to be below him," says Kirby.

Interestingly enough, Kirby told me that when he is calling to a tom on the side of a slope or ridge and the tom is either uphill or downhill from the calling position, the bird almost never comes in diagonally on a beeline to the hunter. Rather, the gobbler's tendency is to approach at a constant line of elevation (on the bird's original level) either above or below the hunter until the tom reaches a point where he can make almost a 90-degree turn and either drop straight down or go straight up to the calling hunter. To the extent this applies, it can help the caller know which direction to face and where to set up, or where to position a partner for whom he may be doing the calling.

As we consider this matter of positioning, we would be remiss if we didn't examine one of the essential differences between the terrain in Western turkey country and the terrain in Eastern or Southern habitats.

Western turkey country is usually hilly, if not downright mountainous, and that's an advantage in being able to move without being seen. As far as we know, no gobbler can see through a hillside. In that respect, up-and-down Western topography certainly is not unique when compared to the ridges and mountains of some states in the East. But mountain turkeys in the West seem inclined to migrate more than other birds. They winter in one area that is lower in elevation than their spring and summer habitat, then move back to higher haunts at the onset of spring. In the very early part of the spring season they may be somewhere in between.

The chief difference in the West is that the ground cover is more sparse. Because of the open terrain, binoculars can be an important accessory. Dense forests (except for some zones of scrub oak and pines) are an exception, not a rule, and low-growth brush and tree cover is thinner and scarcer simply because the climate and soil is drier. The hard, dry ground does not sprout like a fungus-covered dish. Movement into position to call to a gobbler must be done either under the cover of predawn darkness or by way of whatever cover does exist—brush, boulders, ridges, grass, weeds, trees, creek bottoms. Crawl if necessary, and don't assume that camo clothing will mask your movements if you remain upright as you move. If you can see half a mile, so can the turkeys. Even in the darkness before dawn, if there is moonlight, walking shouldn't be done out in the open near a roosted gobbler.

In the West, if you must cross an open area during the day, make the automatic assumption that you are being seen by turkeys that you can't see and conclude that when you do stop walking, some time (at least fifteen minutes) will have to pass before any calling can be effective in that particular spot.

In whatever region he's hunting, a hunter sometimes is caught flat-footed when he suddenly hears or sees a gobbler that is close by, and he has no choice but to sit or lie down right on the spot. But knowing the path a gobbler is likely, or unlikely, to take gives a clue, if nothing else, on just which direction to face.

In cover that is relatively dense, it helps if there's some open, or relatively open, ground in front of or slightly to one side of the caller—open ground that he can cover with his gun. Not only does this make it easier to see an oncoming bird, but a gobbler prefers to have some open space in which he can make his splendid display easily visible to the hen he thinks he hears. Although a tom may refuse to cross a county road or a highway to come to a call, he may in fact be inclined to walk straight down a narrow logging road or open trail simply because it's easy to walk there and he knows he can be seen by the hen.

But hunters in the West are somewhat spoiled. They are so used to relatively open terrain that when they do have to set up in thick cover to call a gobbler (perhaps on a hunt while visiting a Southern state), they get uneasy about it. But it's better to settle for a less than ideal calling spot than to be seen trying to move to a better one. By contrast, Eastern and Southern hunters are used to having relatively restricted areas of vision in front of them and feel reasonably comfortable having a limited field of fire.

The ultimate advantage in this positioning game is to know where the turkey is inclined to go in the first place. I first learned this lesson very indelibly early in my spring-turkey-hunting experience. On a hunt in Texas along the upper Brazos River north of Abilene, a partner and I sat down at one end of a grove of pecan trees along the river and began to call while it was still half-dark. The chorus of gobbles and yelps that greeted our introductory offerings was indicative of what still sticks in my mind as the single largest concentration of roosted Rio Grande turkeys I have ever heard.

But a half hour later, after we traded clucks, yelps, and cackles back and forth with this avian army, not a single turkey—hen, jake, or mature gobbler—had so much as walked in our direction. We learned later that these birds, upon flying down, always went downstream along the river before climbing up to adjacent bluffs, not upstream (which is where we were). By the time we caught on, the weather had deteriorated so badly that further hunting was futile.

On one of my recent hunts in Colorado, the younger of my two sons, Slater, observed a big Merriam's gobbler walking down a rut-road trail in an open pasture about 100 yards out from the base of a ridge. As Slater watched him eventually progress out of sight, he noticed that the tom walked within 30 yards of the ruin of an old stone-walled dugout storage structure used long ago by ranch hands on this vast property in southern Colorado. The crumbled walls were maybe 2 feet high, which would allow a hunter to lie down behind one of them if that happened to be the calling spot he chose. But the ruin was out in the open, and Slater concluded that the tom had originally been roosted about a quarter mile up the valley floor in some creekside cottonwood trees where the base of the continuing ridge was close to the roost trees.

That night, he decided that in the morning he would walk in the predawn darkness up the rut road to the stone-wall ruin, then turn slightly left and go uphill into the rocks and juniper bushes along the lower slope of the ridge. There, he figured he would continue under cover of the junipers and pussyfoot along to within calling distance of the creekside cottonwood trees, where he would be closer to where he expected the tom to be roosting. He wouldn't be so potentially detectable as he might be if crouching or lying behind a low stone wall out in the open. Besides, when he's calling (like most of us) he prefers to sit, not lie down.

At dawn, his first hen yelps drew an answer from the tom. That was the proverbial good news. The bad news was that the gobbler was roosted farther downstream, *between* him and the old stone ruin. Slater had been eminently successful in his efforts to keep his getting-into-position movements a secret from the tom, but he had walked too far if the tom decided to go in the direction he had gone the day before.

Which is exactly what this gobbler did. He flew down, walked straight across the pasture grass to reach the rut road, and instead of turning right to go in the direction of Slater's pleading hen yelps, this wise old bird turned left and went straight down the road, almost exactly in the tracks he had left the day before.

"That rascal walked right past the stone ruin, just where he did yesterday, no more than twenty yards from where I could have been waiting for him if I'd hidden behind the ruin," Slater marveled, shaking his head.

Sometimes we don't outsmart the bird. We outsmart ourselves.

The lesson is fairly simple: For proper positioning, if we know the tendency of a bird or group of birds to go in a certain direction or to a certain place, the spot to be is somewhere along that route or in that specific place. Once I killed a gobbler who had a harem of five hens because I had determined that they were using a particular meadow to feed in. What they were doing was foraging along in the grass, which had been chewed down the previous year by cattle. The cattle had been moved off somewhere else under the normal pasture-rotation routine, but they had left behind a wealth (if that's the right word) of dried-out cow pies. The turkeys were scuffling along, scratching through the dried manure to get to the grubs and larvae that were underneath. I found some tree cover on the edge of the pasture, took a position there, and had to wait no more than forty-five minutes for the feeding party to show up.

In an early morning roost-tree scenario, it may become necessary to position yourself, or reposition yourself, not according to where the gobbler or gobblers may be but according to where the *hens* are. If the hens are on the far side of the gobblers from your position, you have two choices: You can either try to outcall the real hens, or you can try, if there's time and the right cover is available to mask your movements, to circle around and get on the other side of the hens. But if you begin calling and it becomes abundantly clear that the gobbler is going in the direction of, or with, the hens, staying rooted like a swamp cypress is likely to get you nothing but calling practice.

As for the exact hiding spot in which you set up before you utter a henlike cluck, you can probably get a roundly contested debate started over whether this should be a tree trunk, a clump of brush, a deadfall tree, a painstakingly constructed blind using whatever happens to be available, or one of those portable netting-type box blinds.

Personally, I am not one who uses or favors portable blinds. For one thing, they just represent something additional I have to carry. For another, I've never been sure that their rather predictable-looking shapes and contours, however believably they may be camouflaged, don't look unnatural to the turkey.

Preferably, you want to have some sort of cover, something to break up your silhouette, in front of you, such as naturally growing weeds or low bushes, or a pile of dead limbs. This isn't always possible, since you may not have the time to gather this stuff and position it yourself before the turkey shows up. But for those occasions when you do have the time, it's smart to carry a pocketknife with which to whittle down the stems of, say, tall weeds, short scrub brush, or palmetto stalks and sharpen the bases of the stems for sticking in the ground in front of you.

In addition to the time factor, the problem may be a shortage of such material in the immediate area. If all else fails, simply sit back against a sizeable tree trunk, stump, log, or brush clump. There is the added bonus of a safety factor in sitting down against a solid piece of cover such as a tree trunk. Though you're not in an up-against-the-wall-you-redneck-mothers bar brawl situation, you are in the act of sounding like a turkey, and at least you have the comfort of knowing that a load of No. 4s from some dodo isn't going to plow through a tree trunk and nail you in the back. And, presumably, you can see what's out in front of you.

There are some hunters who don't have faith in the camouflage potential of simply sitting up against a bare tree trunk, but the fact is that there are tree-bark-camo clothing patterns on the market now that are so realistic I doubt a woodpecker can tell the difference at 30 yards. Assuming you are properly camo-clad, motion is your worst enemy, not shape.

Important as it is to get in the *right* position, avoiding the wrong one is equally vital. Don't get too close to roosting birds, for instance. Don't press your luck. Gobbler locaters such as owl hooters can help you avoid this pitfall when you are approaching trees in the early morning darkness or dimness. Even if you know the precise tree of an individual roosting tom from having watched him go to roost or heard him the evening before, don't blunder through other trees on the way to him without at first owl-hooting. There may be other gobblers that are nearer to you, and they often will answer an owl hoot. Of course, there's the chance that they won't answer. But if you don't try a locater call, you take the risk of flushing them off the roost or launching them on a loud putting-alarm binge that alerts every other bird in the area.

To sum this sermon up, camouflage and calling expertise certainly are important ingredients in the recipe for hunting success, and they sometimes can overcome poor calling position. Most of the time, however, it is the hunter assuming a well thought out position who finds himself in the catbird seat.

16

YES, TOTO, WE ARE IN KANSAS

I TAGGED THE RIO GRANDE GOBBLER and stood there for a while marveling at the gleaming bronze overtones of his feathering, the white band at the tip of his tail, the bushy 8-inch beard. I was less than three hours into my first Kansas turkey hunt and I was almost sorry it was over, although those three hours had been all any turkey caller could hope for.

I hoisted the 18-pound bird over my shoulder and walked the quarter mile down the old rut road along the edge of the grain-stubble field to my parked vehicle. I laid the gobbler in the grass and lit a cigarette.

A pickup truck turned into the field, drove up, and stopped. The farmer who owned the land got out, said hello, and asked, "Any luck?"

I showed him the gobbler lying behind the vehicle. The grizzled old farmer took a cursory glance at it.

"Is there much to this turkey hunting?" he asked. He explained that he didn't hunt anymore and never had hunted turkeys.

"There is to me," I said, after considering a longer explanation and rejecting the idea.

"Well, we sure got 'em around here," he said, and the rest of the conversation drifted to the dry weather, the fact that the winter wheat crop had all but failed because of the winter-long drought, and that the deer were getting so thick they were trampling and eating the crops the drought didn't destroy. I thanked the farmer for allowing me to hunt on his land and he got back in his truck to tend to his Saturday morning chores.

My two partners on this hunt were somewhere farther up the gravel road that paralleled the nearby creek, a Republican River tributary near the town of Atwood. We had agreed that if I took a turkey early I would drive upstream along the creek bottom and look for their vehicle, and we would get back together sometime in late morning, depending on what the other two hunters had done.

In a 9-mile drive up that road on a lush, sunlit April morning, I counted a total of eighty-four turkeys in scattered small bunches feeding in open fields just out from the cottonwood trees that paralleled the winding creek. Each bunch had at least one strutting gobbler. I wondered how many other turkeys I wasn't able to see simply because they were out of easy view from a passing vehicle. I noticed exactly two other vehicles that looked like they were occupied by spring turkey hunters.

Incredible, I thought: We were hunting in northwestern Kansas, an area that twenty-five years earlier didn't have a single wild turkey in it. For that matter, neither did the rest of the state. Just seventeen years earlier there wasn't even a hunting season on Kansas turkeys. The turkey population in 1966, when Kansas, with a shipment of birds obtained from the King Ranch in Texas, launched its turkey restoration effort, stood at zero. And it had stood there for almost a century. There are records indicating that the last confirmed sighting of a wild turkey in the state previous to the restoration effort was in 1871.

Today, most locals in Kansas think no more of seeing a drove of turkeys than they do of spotting a cock pheasant. There are, by some estimates, as many as 200,000 turkeys of varied lineage in the state population—Rio Grandes, Easterns, and hybrids of the two—and the spring harvest has reached the 15,000-bird level. Hunter success rates are in the rarified realm of anywhere from 40 to 50 percent, unheard of in most other turkey-hunting states. Despite all this, much of the turkey-hunting world has yet to discover Kansas.

To a Coloradan getting his first taste of Kansas turkey hunting, the revelation is nothing short of stunning. Northwestern Kansas long has been viewed as something of an upland bird hunter's paradise by those of us who live in the more arid, less bird-rich climes to the west, but until fairly recent years the object of our envy was the ring-necked pheasant. Or, in the central sections of Kansas, the bobwhite quail. The northwestern farm towns of St. Francis, Atwood, Goodland, and Colby long have been synonymous in many minds with pheasant-hunting heaven. There is even a town along U.S. 36 between St. Francis and Atwood named Bird City.

That name has taken on a new meaning. Almost any small town in Kansas now could be called Turkey City.

If one had to pick a microcosm of the incredibly successful nationwide efforts to bring the American wild turkey back from the shadows of near-extinction, Kansas would be as impressive an example as any, although there are many others. From Vermont to New

York to Virginia to Alabama to Texas to Iowa to Wyoming to Idaho to California and many points in between, the wild turkey is doing just fine, thank you. The National Wild Turkey Federation now officially estimates the presence of 4.2 million turkeys in the United States, with Alaska the only state that is devoid of turkeys. When the federation was organized in 1973, the estimate was 1.3 million.

It's scary to think of how close we came to losing them. In those dismal years just prior to World War II, the wild turkey existed in remnant populations mostly in undeveloped, hard-to-reach enclaves of mature forest or other remote backcountry terrain. No one knows how low the total population got, but estimates place it in the neighborhood of 20,000 to 50,000 birds nationwide in the 1930s and 1940s. The wonder now is why, in most states anyway, we kept the hunting seasons open during those bleak times.

When the turmoil and tragedy of the war was over, states could turn their attention and their resources to such previously esoteric matters as saving and restoring our turkey populations. In the ensuing thirty years, several events occurred that had much to do with what we can now point to as one of the truly dramatic wildlife management success stories of this century.

1. Large numbers of Americans gravitated from rural areas to the towns and the cities. The unrestricted slaughter of turkeys for market purposes had mostly stopped by the end of the nineteenth century, if for no other reason than most of the turkeys were gone. But the practice of subsistence killing of turkeys by rural folk had not stopped. A hunter could bait a trench with corn and fire a blast or two into the row of feeding heads and kill several turkeys with a minimum of expended ammunition. Or he simply took a gun with him on a walk in the woods and used it if a turkey happened to turn up. As these folks gave up the backwoods life, and as poaching regulations began to be enforced against those who remained, turkeys got a breather.

2. The initial wave of the clear-cutting of forests for lumber or farming purposes was over. New-growth trees began to take over, and transition zones of cover and food sources for turkeys grew up along the edges of cleared fields, giving turkeys new habitat. The wild turkey proved that it didn't need a pristine forest of two-hundred-year-old trees to survive.

3. After bumbling and stumbling around for years with turkey-transplanting programs involving birds with varying levels of domestic blood and genes, state game and fish agencies finally came to the realization that pen-raised turkeys were not the answer. These nonwild birds after release stupidly fell prey to foxes, coyotes, bobcats, and other predators, or happily wandered down the road to the nearest farmhouse and took up residence with the chickens. Those that survived near farm- and ranch houses were susceptible to avian diseases or already had the diseases when they were released, and they spread them to wild flocks. Or, during severe winters, farm or ranch families took pity on the wild turkeys they saw and put out feed for them, luring them into close contact with domestic fowl that carried diseases. There are turkey biologists who believe that avian diseases of European and Asian origination were a devastating factor in the decline of the American wild turkey.

   As soon as wildlife agencies made the commitment to trap turkeys out of surviving wild flocks and transplant them to suitable habitat, the great turkey restoration effort was under way.

4. Somebody invented a device known as the "cannon net." This contraption consisted of a large net that could be launched with an explosive charge over the heads of a drove of turkeys baited to the site by wildlife officials who hid in nearby blinds and then rushed in to pen up the birds for transport to other areas of the state or to other states in trade

for other species. New flocks that were established in selected areas of a state served as stocking bases for further translocations to still other parts of that state.

5. It was discovered, little by little, that a given subspecies of turkey such as the Rio Grande or Eastern didn't necessarily have to stay in what historically was its native habitat in order to thrive. You could move a subspecies a thousand miles or more away from home, and if the habitat was right, the birds reproduced and thrived.

6. The National Wild Turkey Federation was formed in 1973 and dedicated itself to the restoration and perpetuation of wild turkey resources and habitat, raising money and providing volunteers to assist states in their restoration programs.

7. Spring-season hunting grew in acceptance and popularity. This provided a way for harvest of the male of the species, as opposed to the any-turkey-is-a-good-turkey attitude that prevailed in many states during fall seasons. The male turkey is a wonderfully efficient polygamist who, given a few weeks, can plant his progeny in a significant number of hens. Seasons are structured so as to give him time to do this.

As recently as the early 1980s, Texas, for example, was a state with a wealth of wild turkeys (400,000 or so) but a population of hunters who didn't understand the value, thrill, and challenge of spring hunting. Most turkeys, of either sex and any age, were killed during white-tailed deer seasons as a kind of incidental offshoot of the deer hunt, often by hunters sniping away at them with rifles from deer blinds. Today, tens of thousands of hunters have gravitated to spring seasons in Texas, and landowners who lease their properties for deer hunting are beginning to realize that turkeys hunted in the spring can be almost as lucrative a cash cow as deer hunted in the fall.

Kansas didn't have any wild turkeys in the early 1960s, but it had a few things that were of value to other states that did have turkeys, such as walleyes, prairie chickens, and the seeds of certain wildflowers. The Kansas Department of Wildlife and Parks obtained its first Rio Grande–strain turkeys from Texas in trade for prairie chickens in 1966 and released 125 in several areas in south-central, southwestern, and northwestern Kansas.

Some of those went to the Republican River–Atwood area, where I hunted. Other Rio Grandes were obtained from the state of Oklahoma. Several introductions were made in a southern tier of counties in the late 1960s and early 1970s, including Harper County, Cowley County, and Commanche County.

Bill Hlavachick, of Pratt, retired research biologist for the Kansas Department of Wildlife and Parks, remembers the first release in northwest Kansas.

"It was a cold winter day, snowing, the wind blowing," he said. "We let those poor Texas birds out and they just sort of humped up—they had never seen snow before. I thought right then, 'This will never work up here.' But those birds hung on for a few years and then finally they took off. In those early years, our hopes were a lot smaller than this program turned out to be. Hell, it took off everywhere, and when the Eastern birds were placed up in the northeast, they took off, too.

"We just had a big niche of habitat that wasn't being filled, and now we have turkeys everywhere, including the CRP grasslands and the shelterbelts," Hlavachick marveled. "They didn't need a virgin forest."

The Oklahoma birds brought into Kansas generally fared better than the Texas Rio Grandes. Carroll Lange, of Winfield, Kansas, a district wildlife biologist for the state wildlife agency, believes the Oklahoma birds simply were climatically better adapted to the Kansas weather and breeding season. The onset of breeding seasons is dictated by increasing lengths and intensities of sunlight, the so-called photo period that varies in timing depending on geographical location. The Texas birds marched to a different, more Southern, drummer, and the adjustment to the Kansas climate was tougher.

Lange joined the department in 1973 and began trapping the recently established birds in Harper County and moving them to western parts of the state. Then came the introduction of the Eastern-strain birds (they since have become well established in the eastern one-third of the state). Lange said the first Eastern turkeys, traded from Missouri in exchange for 3,000 pounds of wildflower seeds, were obtained in 1975. In that trade, Kansas got three hundred turkeys, or one turkey for 10 pounds of seed.

Lange believes the introduction of Eastern birds was a major catalyst that really propelled Kansas into the turkey-boom years. The Easterns hybridized with the Rio Grandes. "The cross [between Easterns and Rio Grandes] was explosive genetically," he said.

But turkeys of both subspecies took hold right from the start. Lange remembers making three releases of five Rio Grande hens and two or three gobblers in 1974 and having three flocks of twenty-five to forty birds by the next winter. Nobody had envisioned what would happen eventually. "Our experts in the mid-1970s thought maybe we would have about 6,000 turkeys in Kansas," Lange remembers.

Now, almost three times that many are killed by spring hunters each year.

Kansas offered its first spring season in 1974 with the issuance of about four hundred permits. The harvest was 123 birds and the success ratio was listed at 40 percent. Eventually, Kansas sold its first unlimited, across-the-board spring-season licenses in 1986 and began to allow nonresident hunting in 1987. The following table on page 151 shows how the seasons progressed:

Year	Harvest	Percentage of Success
1974	123	40
1975	139	44
1976	123	39
1977	149	36
1978	196	44
1979	305	46
1980	369	45
1981	482	47
1982	616	44
1983	945	50
1984	1,430	42
1985	1,544	44
1986	2,167	44
1987	2,777	48
1988	3,977	48
1989	4,898	47
1990	4,988	44
1991	6,602	50
1992	8,898	54
1993	7,710	46
1994	13,008	38
1995	14,953	48

Lange believes three elements came together to bring Kansas to prominence as a major turkey state. The fertility and volatility of the crossbreeding between strains of Rio Grande and Eastern turkeys was one.

Second was the abundant availability of winter feed and habitat—many creek and river drainages affording water, cover, and roost trees, bordered by countless grain-stubble fields with crops such as milo, millet, corn, wheat, and soybeans. Winter die-offs of turkeys in Kansas are rare to nonexistent.

Third, in Lange's view, was the strategic way in which he and others in the Kansas agency established their new turkey flocks: with small releases of maybe a half dozen hens accompanied by two or three gobblers, scattered out at 5- to 10-mile intervals. This helped saturate the available habitat with turkeys.

"I've caught and moved close to 4,000 turkeys, and of all the work I and others in the department did," said Lange, "I don't know of any releases that failed."

Dorothy and Toto would be amazed.

17

The Last Word

THERE IS SOMETHING ABOUT HUMAN NATURE (and probably it's a healthy characteristic) that makes it difficult for many of us to believe certain things we haven't either witnessed or experienced ourselves. There was a survey taken of random persons among the U.S. citizenry some time after the first American astronauts landed on the moon, asking what these people thought about the momentous event. I forget the exact number, but the survey showed that a fairly significant number of Americans doubted that it ever happened. They figured it for a hoax concocted through a conspiracy between NASA and the television medium.

I have never doubted that a select few of my fellow Americans have walked on the moon (I helped pay the bill, didn't I?). However, there are some things I have a hard time believing. And some of these relate to turkey-hunting experiences, tactics, and anecdotes that are conveyed in all seriousness to me and other turkey hunters by self-described experts, usually in the form of books or magazine stories. I am sure there will also be readers of this book, who, for reasons of their own, will conclude that some of the events or theories or tactics related herein resemble reality no more closely than a ceramic caricature in the shape of a Wild Turkey bourbon decanter resembles a real gobbler.

I don't question their right to make those judgments. I can only try to assure them that I am a purveyor of words and ideas, but not of bullshit. My theories and convictions are my own, but events or anecdotes depicted in this book are as true and accurate as my memory can recall them.

Theories and personally preferred tactics are another matter. I respect the right of anybody to disagree with my approach to any aspect of turkey-hunting strategy, and I hope he respects mine.

Therefore, when I say that I consider some of what I read about how to hunt turkeys to be mostly thick-sliced bologna, or at best cliché repetition, I make that statement with the cautious caveat that just because I haven't experienced the same thing doesn't mean it hasn't happened to *somebody.*

For instance: This business of beating one's hat or cap against one's leg to simulate the sound of a turkey flying down from the roost. All sorts of questions tumble into my mind like Ping-Pong balls out of a bingo cage.

First of all, why? Presumably, you are not sitting in a tree stand 30 or so feet off the ground, which is the level from which a gobbler would expect to hear wing beats. You are sitting on the ground. How realistic is a wing-beat noise, for example, if it's coming from a clump of brush 100 yards away from the nearest roost tree? Wing beats at ground level would presumably be more likely to signal trouble to a gobbler (another turkey is escaping a predator) than it would the impending appearance of convivial company. If the gobbler is still roosted, he probably can see—a hell of a lot better than you can—any adjacent roost trees where other turkeys might be about to fly down.

Second, what about all this movement you are generating by beating your camouflaged cap against your camouflaged leg? How can a turkey hunter who uses mouth diaphragms, because they allow him to keep his hands from moving, reconcile this precaution with the wild flailing of his arm and hand while he beats a cap against his leg? What is a gobbler to think if he hears fly-down sounds coming from a spot where there is no tree (assuming you have set up somewhere else besides up against a tree trunk)? Surely the sound of a yelping hen is more believable than the beating of wings.

In the same category, I would place the tactic of scratching in the leaves to sound like a feeding turkey. I would think that if a gobbler is close enough to you to hear you scratching in the leaves, he is already pretty damned close to strolling into shotgun range. Presumably, he got that close because you used one or more calling devices to bring him to you. Assuming that's what you did, the gobbler, with his incredible ability to home in on sounds, already knows where the hell you are, give or take 2, 3, 5, 10, or 15 yards. He may know virtually which bush you're hiding behind or tree you're sitting under. The only thing that's puzzling him is why he can't actually distinguish the shape, form, color, and silhouette of a female turkey. What good are hand movement and ground-scratching sounds going to do to assure him that his original conclusion was correct? I would think you are better off offering him some clucks or purrs from a mouth caller and using your hands to point the shotgun.

I once read a story about an expert hunter who makes it a point to "walk through the woods like a turkey." Presumably he tiptoes along, stopping every few feet to reach down and scratch around in the leaves or the dirt. Or maybe he stops and puffs himself up and goes *vritt-vroom,* à la a drumming, strutting gobbler.

What I have yet to read is an explanation of how a human being who stands (on average) somewhere between 5 feet 7 inches and 6 feet 3 inches tall and weighs from 140 to 200 pounds or more shrinks himself down to the size and shape of a turkey. I assume that if you are trying to sound like a walking turkey, you are trying to call attention to yourself as the embodiment of a walking turkey. If you have reason to believe that turkeys are close enough to hear you walking, why the hell are you walking in the first place?

Once I read a story, in what was supposed to be a compendium of hunting-strategy "secrets" from the finest turkey hunters in the land, about a hunter who took off one of his red socks (or reached into his pocket for one he carried for these occasions, I forget which), fitted it over his hand and wrist, lay down behind a tree, and stuck the hand up in the air to look like the head of a gobbler or jake. This "secret" trick, if it ever really happened, strikes me as one of the more reckless and stupid moves ever made by anybody purporting to be a turkey hunter, much less an expert on the subject.

There are some real experts, true professionals, who are now manufacturing and selling calling devices designed to simulate the "fighting purrs" of a couple of gobblers going at it over territory or harem dominance. I withhold judgment on this because I have only heard these noises on films and tapes and I have never used such a call. In other words, I don't have much to go on. And it's certainly possible that aggressive turkey gobblers, or curious turkeys of any sex or age, might respond to combat-type noises just as white-tailed deer respond to the rattling of antlers.

I will continue to plod along with my pedestrian ways, depending on positioning, camouflage, and basic hen-noise calls to accomplish most of my deception. Having said that, I will also say that there is never a hunt that goes by when I don't learn something new about turkeys, and to that extent it will pay me to keep an open mind. Meanwhile, here are some final thoughts on various aspects of hunting wild turkeys.

CAMOUFLAGE

I believe that it makes sense to tailor your choice of camo clothing shades and patterns to the type of cover you are going to be hunting in. If you are doing most or all of your hunting in areas where there are sizeable trees and lots of them, and you do quite a bit of your calling sitting back against the trunks of trees, a tree-bark camo pattern with gray overtones makes sense, as does tree bark mixed with a leaf-overlay pattern. If you are doing most of it in brushy or low-growth leafy areas or palmetto swamps, you may want to wear the basic military-style camouflage with an overtone of green shades. If you are hunting in the fall, when the leaves and weeds are dry and brown, you may want to go with a tan or brownish camo pattern.

It pays to wear camo gloves when calling, even if you have to wear thin gloves in warm or hot weather. Always have some sort of head and face cover in addition to a camo cap, either in the form of a pullover mask or a pull-up veil-type face mask. Avoid wearing white socks. Go with brown, green, or olive drab socks. Inevitably, when you sit down with your knees up, your pants legs are going to hike up and expose the tops of your socks. Finally, it makes sense to cover the shiny barrel and other metal parts of your shotgun with camo tape. If you're worried about aesthetics, you can always remove the tape after the turkey season.

SHOTGUNS

I believe that the best choice in gauges is the 12 gauge, although there is nothing in the laws of physics or ballistics that says you can't kill a turkey with something smaller, such as a 20 gauge. But you are just handicapping yourself with lesser firepower, in my opinion, and increasing the risk of losing a wounded turkey. These birds are too magnificent and too valuable to take chances on not killing them quickly and mercifully. As for striving for maximum fire-power, there are those (and some of them are true experts) who opt for 10 gauge guns. I don't believe these cannons are necessary, and I consider it enough of a chore to walk around with a 12 gauge over-under in my hand all day without having to wear a cannon strapped around my shoulder with a sling.

As mentioned earlier, there are those who think the ideal turkey gun is one with a short barrel. My feeling is that the ultimate object in terms of shooting on a turkey hunt isn't to swing quickly and fire at a running or flying turkey but to carefully sight down, rifle-style, on a stationary or slowly walking bird. A longer barrel offers a truer sighting plane and helps maintain a relatively compact pattern at longer ranges.

LOADS

I will not try to fool anybody by claiming to know anything about the ballistics characteristics of these relatively new "turkey loads" that incorporate a portion of smaller shot sizes mixed with a portion of larger shot sizes. Just what the advantage could be entirely escapes my simple mind, unless it's the hope that if we miss the head and neck with the pattern but connect in the body with some of the larger shot, we still have a chance to kill the turkey.

If a hunter feels he needs the capability of a heavier load for a second or even a third shot at a turkey that is trying to escape, he always has the option of loading, say, a No. 4 or No. 6 as his first shell and backing it up with one or two No. 2 shells, depending on whether he's using a double gun, a pump, or an autoloader.

My choice, using an over-under 12 gauge choked full and modified, is to load a No. 4 or No. 5 shell in both barrels and fire the modified barrel first. I have no quarrel with those who use No. 6 shot on the rationale that it provides a denser pattern and they are head-shooting anyway, therefore they don't need to worry about body-impact loads. But No. 7½ shot is undergunning, in my opinion. I use nothing smaller than No. 5 because, although No. 6

creates a denser pattern, if I miss a vital part of the head or neck, I am a lot more likely to anchor or slow down the turkey with a body or wing shot from No. 4s, for example, than I am with No. 6 shot. After all, we are talking about birds that weigh anywhere from 12 to 25 pounds, with 18 pounds as a pretty good average.

Copper-plated shot as opposed to all-lead? No quarrel there. Theoretically, it lends itself to a more uniform pattern and greater penetration. I just think that before a hunter makes the choice he needs to pattern his shotgun and see what it does at, say, 30 and 40 yards with one as opposed to the other. For that matter, we all ought to have some conception of how our guns pattern with various sizes and types of shot. One gun may pattern better with 4s than with 5s, for example, or vice versa.

CALLING DEVICES

This has been covered in chapter 7, but again, my choices, in order of preference, are one, box, two, mouth diaphragm, and three, slate. I don't believe there is anything that can match the raspy realism of a good box. It should be kept in mind, however, that not all boxes are made out of cedar wood, or out of wood at all. In my experience, nonwooden boxes tend to screech and leave something to be desired in realism. By all means, use what you feel most comfortable with. If that happens to be a wing bone or a willow leaf or a piece of condom stretched over a pill bottle, so be it.

DECOYS

I don't own any turkey decoys, although I have, upon occasion, hunted over them with partners who do. As a matter of personal choice (call it prejudice if you like), I don't choose to use decoys in turkey hunting. For one thing, they make me nervous, particularly when I'm hunting within sight of roads or in heavily pressured public areas. I keep envisioning some yahoo jumping out of his vehicle and firing a rifle at the turkey he thinks he sees, or some nearsighted shotgun hunter stalking the decoy. It probably makes sense, for safety's sake, to position the decoy so that it's not broadside to where you're sitting.

Decoys can make a difference, there's no doubt about it. A decoy may bring a tom in that would otherwise be reluctant to come to a call. But I don't want to go to the bother of carrying one around with me, and there's something about the idea of decoying a gobbler that goes against my grain as a turkey caller. Why I feel this way about decoying turkeys and not about decoying ducks or geese is not something I can easily and coherently explain, but there it is, anyway. I already relish the challenge of calling gobblers, and something that takes the edge off this challenge isn't what I'm looking for. Every hunter has to make his or her own choice about decoys, and I respect whatever that choice is.

CHOOSING A HUNTING AREA

If you have moved to a new state or are just getting started in turkey hunting, it will pay to make contact with your state's fish and game agency. There are turkeys in every state except Alaska, although a few states allow hunting only on a limited-permit basis because of relatively low populations of turkeys.

The wildlife agency should be able to provide you with a map of turkey population densities in your state. You can compare this to, or superimpose it over, a state highway map, land-status map, or topo map and figure out where the turkeys are. Similarly, the agency should have some sort of idea about which counties historically have ranked the highest in turkey harvest, spring and fall. Once you have this data it is a matter either of finding public property (state or federal) on which to hunt or of lining up permission to hunt private land. Two or three days spent knocking on doors in prime turkey country may be well worth the time and effort.

SCOUTING

In my home state there is growing agreement that elk are moving down to winter range much earlier than they historically have and that the cause is the glut of late-summer and early-fall activity surrounding early bow seasons, muzzleloading seasons, bear seasons, and assorted other high-country recreation such as joyriding in ATVs. By the time the main rifle seasons begin, many elk already have been harassed down to private ranch properties and proceed to attack haystacks, pastures, and crops. Ranchers and farmers complain about this, file damage claims with the wildlife agency, and then double dip by charging for hunting.

What does all this have to do with spring turkey hunting? Bear with me. It is my feeling that in many areas of this country, particularly hard-hunted public lands, preseason scouting does more harm than good. All that activity before the season starts can cause turkeys to change their movement patterns and become somewhat call-shy even before the first shot is fired.

The trouble is, no turkey hunter worth his camo face mask is going to go into turkey woods, even before the season, without a calling device or two. And he is, by gobbler, going to use it. To me this seems roughly equivalent to walking through a pheasant field the day before the season starts to see how many birds you can flush.

I confine my on-the-ground scouting to the actual hunting season. In a new area I do a lot of moving around, calling periodically but also looking for sign. Preseason scouting might better consist, if you can find cooperative people, of talking to other hunters or landowners who are familiar with the area you will be hunting.

FALL SEASONS

I purposely didn't devote any previous space to this subject because I am not a fan of fall turkey hunting, much less an expert on it. To me, the essence and the excitement of turkey hunting is calling to individual gobblers in the spring. In the fall, gobblers are either with large fall-winter droves (flocks) numbering anywhere from thirty to up in the hundreds or hanging out in three- or four-bird bachelor groups that are second only to hermit gobblers in terms of being tough to call. Admittedly, in this context, fall-season calling directed at older bachelor gobblers is even more of a challenge than spring-season calling. I have great respect for those who can do it. But it's also an undertaking that may be somewhat similar to trying to hit a three-team parlay in betting college football. It can be done, but it doesn't necessarily make for consistent results.

Many hunters in the fall are content to stumble on or ambush droves of turkeys and pick one out of the bunch to shoot. Others insist on calling in their turkeys, and they generally do this by busting up sizeable droves (either by running toward them and shouting or by firing a shotgun over their heads), waiting a little while, then trying to call some of the scattered flock back together. There is a skill and even an art to this scattering business, and I don't belittle it for a moment—it just isn't my style. But if you can call a lone hermit gobbler or a small group of old bachelor gobblers into gun range in the fall, I tip my hat to you and the drinks are on me.

In the fall, it's feast or famine in locating turkeys. If you find one, you usually find a lot of them all in the same place. But because they are flocked up, there's an awful lot of terrain out there that won't have any turkeys in it. Hiking long distances can definitely be a big part of fall hunting.

One aspect of fall hunting that I don't favor is the fact that in many fall hunting states it is legal to take either a hen or a tom. Much of what gets taken home turns out to be young toms (poults) born that spring, or hens. But there is a major difference between a four- to six-month-old poult and a yearling gobbler (jake) that weighs 14 or 15 pounds the following spring.

I don't have any fallacious concern that killing hens in the fall will devastate the turkey populations, although in marginal population areas it certainly can't help. It's more a feeling that we are better off in the long run taking only male birds, and I feel a sense of insecurity in knowing that there are some fall hunters out there who don't care whether what they shoot is a hen or a gobbler. If they don't care what kind of turkey it is, my fear is that they may not be looking closely enough to make sure it's a turkey in the first place.

GETTING STARTED

Books, instructional tapes, and videos are good starting points, but it's hard to beat having a friend who is an experienced turkey hunter. If he takes you under his wing, you are going to be privy to more inside information than you might ever get if you asked the same favor of, say, a bass fisherman or a deer hunter. It's my conviction that turkey hunters love their sport so much that being secretive about any aspect of it (with the exception of keeping private hunting spots private) is as foreign to their nature as robbing banks or hoarding pennies.

It won't hurt, either, to join the National Wild Turkey Federation, the not-for-profit organization that, since 1973, has dedicated itself to the perpetuation, conservation, and continued growth of wild turkey populations. Their publications, including the magazine *Turkey Call,* offer a combination of education, entertainment, research, and news that can't be easily obtained from any other single source. Joining a local chapter of the federation, if there's one available in your area, will put you in contact with others of your persuasion who will share with you their knowledge and insights and appreciate your doing the same for them. The national headquarters address is National Wild Turkey Federation, P. O. Box 530, Edgefield, SC 29824-1510; (803) 637-3106.

Go ye therefore and seek the wild turkey. You will find yourself in some of the most beautiful settings on earth at some of the most gorgeous times of the year, becoming intimate with the most challenging, intriguing, spellbinding quarry a hunter can hope to pursue.

Good luck and good hunting. And listen closely when you open those rusty, squeaky gates.

Swingblade Flip&Zip
         800 - 447 - EDGE